GUMBOOTS IN

Caitlin Press Inc.
3375 Ponderosa Way
Qualicum Beach, BC V9K 2J8
www.caitlinpress.com

Text and cover design by Vici Johnstone
Edited by Lou Allison
Printed in Canada

Cover image *Millionaires*. Photo Rick James courtesy Anita Hamilton
Illustration on page 1 by Joe Ziner. Illustration on back cover by Joe Ziner.

"Ancestor" was previously published in *Rotary Sushi: many kinds of stories & 5 translations by Mihiro Kizuki*, Hillel Wright (New Orphic Publishers: Nelson, BC), 2003.

Caitlin Press Inc. acknowledges financial support from the Government of Canada and the Canada Council for the Arts, and the Province of British Columbia through the British Columbia Arts Council and the Book Publisher's Tax Credit.

Gumboots in the straits : nautical adventures from Sointula to the Salish Sea / edited by
   Lou Allison with Jane Wilde.
Allison, Lou, editor. | Wilde, Jane, 1955- compiler.
Series statement: Gumboot series ; 4
Canadiana 20240376323 | ISBN 9781773861548 (softcover)
LCSH: Men—British Columbia—Pacific Coast—Biography. | LCSH: Urban-rural migration—British Columbia—History—20th century. | LCSH: Country life—British Columbia—Pacific Coast. | LCSH: Seafaring life—British Columbia—Pacific Coast. | LCSH: Pacific Coast (B.C.)—Biography. | LCGFT: Biographies.
LCC HQ1090.7.C2 G86 2024 | DDC 305.31092/27111—dc23

GUMBOOTS
in the STRAITS

Nautical Adventures from
Sointula to the Salish Sea

Edited by Lou Allison
with Jane Wilde

CAITLIN PRESS 2024

Contents

Surge Narrows. Photo Claudia Lake

Cape Caution

Queen Charlotte Strait

Kingcome Inlet

Cape Scott

Broughton Strait

Malcolm Island

Broughton Archipelago

Port Hardy

Swanson Island

Quatsino

Port McNeil

Sointula

Cormorant Isl.

Johnstone Strait

Sayward Kelsey Bay

Vancouver Island

Quadra Island

Surge Narrows

Tahsis

Quathiaski Cove

Nuchatlitz

Nootka Sound

Estevan Point

Tofino

This map is for reference only. Not for navigation.

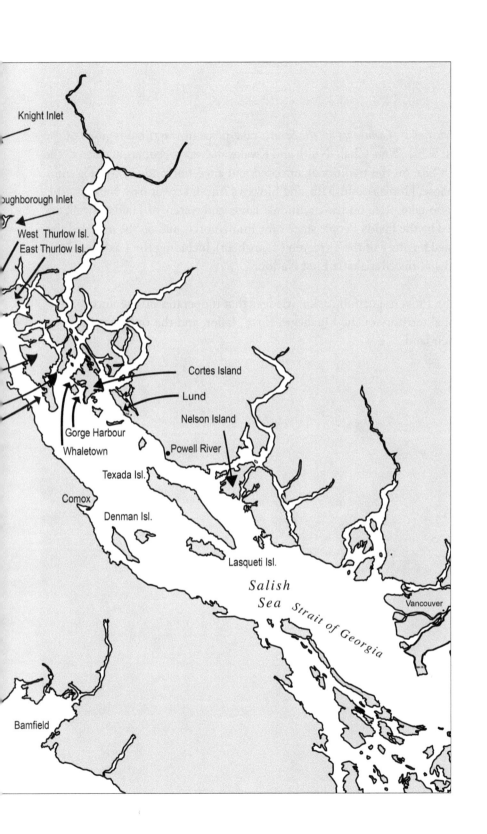

Knight Inlet

oughborough Inlet

West Thurlow Isl.
East Thurlow Isl.

Cortes Island

Lund

Nelson Island

Gorge Harbour

Whaletown

Powell River

Texada Isl.

Comox

Denman Isl.

Lasqueti Isl.

Salish Sea *Strait of Georgia*

Vancouver

Bamfield

The stories in *Gumboots on the Straits* take place in the tribal regions of the Coast Salish, Nuu-Chah-Nulth and Kwakwaka'wakw Peoples, and across the Salish Sea, on the traditional, unceded and ancestral lands of the Tla'amin, Klahoose, Homalco, shíshálh, and Skwx̱wú7mesh Úxwumixw Nations. Stories also take place on the traditional lands and waters of Haida Gwaii, occupied by the Haida People since time immemorial, and on the unceded traditional territory of the Ts'msyen (Tsimshian), including the Lax Kw'alaams Band and the Metlakatla First Nation.

Caitlin Press respectfully acknowledges that it operates on the unceded traditional territory of the Qualicum First Nation and the traditional keepers of their land.

Alert Bay Docks, 1970s. Photo Bill Wilby, Alert Bay Museum

Jane's Introduction

Thanks to the willingness of another twenty-five people to jump in and share their stories from the seventies, we have a second collection of stories about men and boats. Their openness to looking back fifty years to share memories with us is appreciated. I have been moved by the unique combinations of toughness and vulnerability.

Thanks Paul Bozenich, Roger Purdy, John Thorington and Joe Ziner for your help in finding these writers, writing your own stories and encouraging our group process as it unfolded this winter and spring.

Fish boats, sailboats, freighters and kayaks are all here. The good-looking young fellows with their endless energy, strength, curiosity and hair are here too, along with their fearlessness and chance taking. The friends, lovers, children, family, mentors and boat captains of those years also feature in their stories.

We came of age in the sixties and seventies, a time of big world and personal life changes for many of us. We shared motivations that drew many of us to the BC Coast from across North America. Some US Vietnam war resisters moved north and to the coast, for a new political environment. Adventures, life changes, boating and commercial fishing, self-sufficient farming, tree planting and logging, opportunities and work of all sorts were easy to find in those years.

Now we are in our sixties, seventies and eighties. Our lives have shifted, we've moved around some more, gone after new adventures, lost touch with each other, and lost friends and partners. At the same time the connections remain and our books bring that all back together for us. The individuals and communities that supported us show up again for us in these words and photos.

Historian and friend Jo Mrozewski has spurred me on, opened my eyes to the importance of continuing to save our stories and photos as our own, important, pieces of Canadian social history.

Chris Armstrong at Muskeg Press started this Gumboot thing with us, and Vici Johnstone at Caitlin Press keeps it going.

Lou Allison, thanks for saying yes again to Book Four. Who knew we'd still be hanging out like this after meeting in Queen Charlotte City/Daajing Giids in 1976, almost fifty years ago?

Endless thanks and love to my dear family and friends for the support and encouragement that mean everything to me. I couldn't have kept compiling without you.

Lou's Introduction

In 2011, when we embarked on putting together a book for a lark, we never dreamed the journey that lay ahead. This book is the fourth in what has become a series. Jane Wilde's initial idea of gathering the stories of young women who came to the North Coast of BC in the seventies, part of a continent-wide demographic shift, keeps gathering momentum, with new twists along the way. Book Three, *Gumboot Guys*, about the young men who became smitten with boats after they arrived in that same time and place, has led to this collection of stories from the Straits area (Salish Sea to Sointula and beyond). Same, only different: same time frame, similar but not identical geography, stories that are linked but not conjoined.

Once again, I would like to thank the writers, who dug into their memories, and often their emotions, to write deeply personal stories. An unexpected benefit was hearing from so many of them that they rekindled old relationships and revisited a time in their life when all seemed possible, that they involved their friends and families in the process, and above all that they enjoyed the challenge. What a gift!

Thank you to Jane, once again, for your inspirational leadership and organizational skills. You well know that when you call, the answer will be "yes" because you make it all so much fun.

Lou and Jane

Albatross II, Duckling and Blue Comet

Tony Berger

In 1972, my wife, Donna, and I left the winter blizzards of Regina, Saskatchewan, behind for the warm Chinook winds of Calgary to pursue our professional careers. Two years later, we moved to Ladner in green British Columbia in search of our "back to the land" dream. After searching in the Interior and the Gulf Islands, we ventured up the coast to Sointula on Malcolm Island, and finally settled in Mitchell Bay. We met many "conscientious objectors" who had already found land and were working at seasonal jobs like tree planting with the local TreeSing Co-op. Young women and men worked much like the original Finn settlers had, following their emancipated ideals of equal pay for equal work. Several of us in Mitchell Bay bought a cedar shake mill. We cut and sold shakes and helped to put a shake roof on the Sointula Community Hall.

In 1976, my wife and I paddled our canoe to Alert Bay. While walking along the docks we found the *Miss Andrea*, a seiner, short of a crewman. The

Looking over the wheelhouse heading down Johnstone Strait.

skipper and his wife took a chance on a prairie greenhorn and my fishing career began. The crew was extremely helpful and taught me the ropes and kept me safe as a skiff man. I would take my 109 Land Rover to catch the early morning ferry to Alert Bay every Sunday to help prepare for the weekly three- or four-day fishing opening. What an adventure!

During that year I noticed a classic antique gillnetter, the *Albatross II*, tied up inside the Alert Bay breakwater, all painted and ready to go. I just fell in love with it! The owner was a successful businessman who owned the ShopRite store. My wife, expecting our first child, and I approached him to purchase the boat, then went to the Alert Bay Credit Union and secured our first boat loan. The manager approved the loan just on faith.

I had never been aboard a gillnetter but a mechanic who had been making a weekly Sunday night dark set with it agreed to teach me the mechanics and how to set the net.

The *Albatross II* was a twenty-nine-foot double-ender, built in Sointula, with a two-cylinder Vivian engine. One of the last "putt putt" engines that could be heard miles from shore. The wheelhouse was tiny, and the bench seat sat over the open, noisy engine. It was best to stand outside and look

Albatross II tied behind fish packer *Naomi W* at the Mitchell Bay dock.

over the wheelhouse. It didn't have a radar. When the fog rolled into Johnstone Strait, I remembered an old-timer's advice, "head for the shore, tie up
to the bull kelp and go to sleep."

Learning the tides and currents, especially around Blackney Passage,
was a challenge and I found my net "endo" many times. The local gillnetters
and others helped me a lot. In the early season the fishing fleet headed north
to Prince Rupert, and we had the straits to ourselves.

As it turned out Mitchell Bay was a perfect location. There was a day
camp for Gulf trollers run by Seafood Products. Cathy Turner operated the
camp, and her husband, Spence, ran the packer *Naomi W.* The airways re-
sounded with Spence's famous "okey dokey" as he made the morning rounds
collecting the gillnetters' catches.

After three years I bought the *Duckling*, a local gillnetter. It had a Bed-
ford diesel engine, but was a spec boat, built on the Fraser River. I realized
that it needed some repair. One winter I leased a boatshed and hired a shipwright, Pat Brown, a newcomer to Sointula. He agreed to a lower wage but
insisted on working six days a week and ten hours a day. We found more rot
than expected. The shed's owner would often join us with his morning coffee,
penknife in hand, and he would find yet more rotten planks. I freaked, but his
comeback was: "It's not a problem, it's an opportunity."

Launching the rebuilt *Duckling* with family and Pat Brown.

We rebuilt the *Duckling* stem to stern and keel to decks and above! Years later I realized the shed owner was right. Working with the shipwright, I had learned about woodworking, fibreglass, hydraulics and more. We even turned it into a combination troller-gillnetter. I was able to pass this knowledge on to my son Sasha when he worked on his fishing boats.

The *Duckling* had more living space and my family joined me on fishing trips to Rivers and Smith Inlets. My neighbour and friend Jerry Johnson fished the *Southern Slope*, a family-built gillnetter. He was the best travelling partner and mentor, teaching me the rest of the coast. He also fished with his children and grandchildren.

One of our children's favourite times was dark set time. I would steer the boat along the cork line, and they would sit on the trunk cabin holding a handheld spotlight, counting the silver flashes of the salmon.

One year while in Smith Inlet, I was so tired after multiple days of fishing that I had the kids tend to the net while I had a nap, agreeing to let them have the catch. *Wow*—it was the biggest set of the week! They were so proud and hooked on the thrill of fishing.

One year in Jones Cove in Smith Inlet, I met a Japanese fisherman who, like so many, retired at age sixty-five and sold me his boat, the *Blue Comet*. With a bigger boat we ventured north to the Nass and Skeena Rivers. On big fish cycles the price of fish dropped, so we dressed our catch and ran fresh fish to the Steveston Fish Sales Dock. We then got a fair price, but a lot of extra work. We met freezer boats that were able to hold their catch longer. Another opportunity! We turned our gillnetter into a freezer boat. We hired a shipwright in Annieville Slough on the Fraser River to refit our gillnetter. Far Excel Refrigeration with Hans Elfert installed the flash freezer. My children and I fished along the coast and sold our frozen catch at Steveston for ten years. Quality Sashimi Salmon: it turned into a full-time fishing business.

Sasha bought his first boat *Summer Wages* at age nineteen. My daughter Carly was the best deckhand ever. We made a great team. After that we ventured into another opportunity by selling "value added" fillets, smoked and canned fish, at the Vancouver farmers' markets as Blue Comet Seafoods.

At seventy-seven, I'm still fishing a few openings on the coast, catching salmon for the fresh fish market and freezing the rest. My new wife, Donna Fay, enjoys deckhanding, along with my grandson Ethan. They see this as an adventurous opportunity to see the BC coast. We reside in Mitchell Bay, and both have a passion for gardening with a strong community of organic gardeners.

Ancestor

Hillel Wright, 1943-2017

22 October, 1979. Baynes Sound, Denman Island Wharf.
0300 hours, wind southeast, 30–40 knots.

0345 hours, wind southeast, 15–20 knots, rainy.
0600 hours, wind southeast, 10–20 knots, hard rain.

Oystering. Time and tide wait for no one. It's now or never. I get up and light a
fire in the wood-burning cookstove.

0715 hours, wind southeast, 10-15 knots, rain.

The crew, Achmed Kassim Sirouk, deckhand, and Richard Clark, oysterman with the Fanny Bay Oyster Company, our charter, arrive from Buckley Bay. I meet them at the ferry landing and get the latest forecast from the ferry skipper. Strong southeast winds, twenty-five knots to gale-force winds of thirty-five knots are predicted.

Ancestor is a good sea boat. A forty-foot wooden sailboat, it was built in the Eastern Caribbean and sailed in the Windward Islands and the Guianas, freighting and smuggling. It was sold to a Canadian, Jon Van Tamelin, in 1975, and he sailed it to British Columbia with stone ballast via the Panama Canal, the Galapagos and Hawaii. Shortly after arriving on the BC coast he sold it to fisherman Leif Arntzen and I bought it from him in December 1978. In the spring of 1979, I equipped it with a three-cylinder Isuzu diesel linked to a seventeen-inch wheel. This was, at best, auxiliary power. *Ancestor* was not built with engine power in mind, but was powerfully rigged as a gaff cutter with a six hundred square foot mainsail, a club-footed staysail, and a working jib on a ten-foot bowsprit. We steered by tiller joined to a hardwood rudderpost, pumped by hand, and had no electronic, not even a radio.

But *Ancestor* was sound and seaworthy and we had a crew of three strong men. Kassim was known around the docks as "the hydraulic winch," and spent a lot of time arm wrestling in pubs. We had about thirty-five nautical miles to Cortes Bay, where we could hole up overnight. With a strong wind, even a gale behind us all the way, we should make it in six hours. Besides Comox Harbour, ten miles northwest up Baynes Sound, there was no other reliable shelter until we crossed the Strait of Georgia.

We spent a couple of hours stowing and securing the gear needed for a ten-day oystering trip to the southeast side of Cortes Island. We left the wharf at 9:45. The wind was down to a moderate breeze, eight to ten knots southeast, but the sky was dark and the cloud bellies ragged. We ran up Baynes Sound under full mainsail, staysail and jib. We had Union Point on Vancouver Island abeam to

Day sailing a Davidson skiff off of Denman Island.

port at 10:15. A strong sudden gust struck the sails and I had to lean hard into the tiller to prevent a jibe. Kassim and Richard went forward to take in the headsails. By 10:45, as we approached Comox bar, the wind had increased to a steady twenty-five knots and was beginning to gust higher. We lined up the range lights for crossing the bar and steered north-northeast to keep us in the narrow passage between the shoals off the White Spit on the Denman Island side and the rocks off of Willemar Bluffs approaching Cape Lazo on Vancouver Island. We started the engine for auxiliary power. We were on a beam reach and the *Ancestor* rolled heavily into the choppy channel, but "a rolling boat will always see you through" and by 11:45 we had passed Buoy P57 off the cape and were steeling northeast by compass for Sutil Point on Cortes Island, seventeen nautical miles away.

Now was the time to take a deep reef in the main. We had broken a skylight window in the cabin roof while crossing the bar and we had a leaky thru-hull fitting below. The wind in the gulf was now gale strength and *Ancestor* was getting harder and harder to keep on course. I worried about whether the rudderpost would hold and I wanted to patch the skylight, plug the thru-hull fitting, and pump.

We came into the wind, using the engine to hold us in place while we cast off the main halyard and the two gaff halyards. When the huge sail was

A lull in the wind.

halfway down the mast, big trouble struck. One of the gaff halyards kinked and stuck itself in a donut-shaped fairlead on a spreader bar, about thirty feet above the deck. I gave Richard the helm and ran up the ratlines to try and free the line, while Kassim attempted to bag the wet, heavy sail. I was a few feet below the spreader bar when a strong gust hit the sail belly, which snapped Kassim over the side into the cold, grey, choppy sea.

The next fifteen minutes seemed like half an eternity. I shouted for Richard to "keep pointing!" at Kassim as I shoved the engine up to full throttle and took over the helm. We were just able to lower the *Ancestor*'s monstrous boom into a carved notch in the boom gallows on the back deck, ready the life-ring, which hung from a hook on the gallows, and throw Kassim a life jacket. He got the jacket on, but he had drifted beyond the range of the life-ring. We had to turn the *Ancestor* and try again.

At this point, Kassim told us later, he feared that the ship would run him over. His whole life literally flashed before his eyes and he was filled with a great love for both Richard and myself and he prayed that we would be alright and survive the storm.

"I can't see him!" I heard Richard shouting.

Miraculously, the whole time our ordeal was going on, a small private floatplane was hastily retreating to Courtenay to land on the river. I guess we all saw Kassim in his yellow Helly Hansen raingear and orange life-vest

Napping through the afternoon doldrums.

at the same time. Richard waved at the plane and pointed to Kassim in the water, and then the plane dipped its wings in response. We threw the life-ring again and this time Kassim scrambled into it and we began to pull him back to the boat.

A few minutes later a red and white C-113 Labrador helicopter from CFB Comox appeared above us. The floatplane had deciphered Richard's signals and radioed for help.

We soon had Kassim alongside the *Ancestor*. He weighed 240 pounds dry, but now, soaking wet and numb with cold, he was dead weight in the water. We signaled the helicopter and began to let out our lifeline. Kassim drifted away from us in the ring until he was far enough away for the chopper to hover and send down a rescuer on a cable to pick Kassim up. Seconds later, he was lying beside another rescuer in a sleeping bag and was headed for St. Joseph's Hospital in Comox. It was twelve noon.

To make a very long story short, Richard and I managed to get the mainsail down and lashed, and to reset the heavy, self-tending canvas staysail. With the gale blowing harder all afternoon it was about all the power we needed, although we ran the engine at cruising speed to assist while we had the dangerous shoals of Mitlenatch Island as a lee shore. I managed to nail a piece of plywood over the broken skylight pane, plug the leaky thru-hull with the right shaped piece of wood from a box of wood scraps, and pump out enough water from the bilge to stop the nerve-wracking sound of sloshing below deck.

At 1400 hours, the wind was gusting above fifty knots, the sea was smoky and furious, and there was a vicious lump over the Mitlenatch shoals. This was about the worst of it, except that the wind was blowing so hard ahead that we couldn't get out of the channel between Cortes and Twin Islands and into Cortes Bay. We anchored for the night in fifteen fathoms in the lee of Twin Island and made it into Cortes Bay during a brief lull the next morning. The following day, after being watched for signs of hypothermia, Kassim returned, and soon it was back to work, oystering.

A week later, loaded down with 7,000 pounds of oysters, we got ready to return to Baynes Sound. On October 30, at 12:35 p.m., we again pass Buoy P57 off Cape Lazo. The wind is northwest, ten to fifteen knots, the sea slightly choppy, and the sky overcast in the south and clearing in the north. Kassim begins, in Arabic, a Muslim thanksgiving chant—"Allah hu! Allah hu!" Richard, a Christian, and myself, a Jew, join in. "Allah hu! Allah hu! Allah hu!" We are all chanting and dancing joyfully around the deck.

31 October 1979, 1500 hours: Moored. Denman Island wharf. Allah hu!

AnDon, Dovre and Careta II

Jeff Hartbower

Willa Cather wrote, "The end is nothing, the road is all." That has been my credo: focus on the road at my feet and then follow my feet down that road.

Jeff and Jo

Up until 1966, I had used schooling to keep out of the army. Sit in a classroom and be privileged and safe, that's how it worked. This deception bothered me. The Quakers counselled prison as a protest. I needed another way.

I had a diploma that meant little to me, and I was living with a wonderful woman in San Francisco, trying to decide what to do. At the pre-induction army physical, I checked off bed-wetting, cold sweats and nightmares. The army psychiatrist just smiled and said, "Those nightmares will get worse in Vietnam."

A deserter friend mentioned that draft dodgers were going to Canada. Canada? Where was Canada? But crossing that border into Canada was a road taken from the cuckoo's nest into an extraordinary new life.

Jo Swallow and I married to simplify our immigration, and worked at a variety of jobs in Vancouver until we visited friends in Quatsino. To get there, we took our first trip on a BC ferry to Vancouver Island, and our first ride on a fishboat to the village of Quatsino. From then on everything would be a first. We were awed by the expanse of trees and sky and choppy grey water under low clouds that rained the whole time we were there. We were awed by the people who didn't seem to notice the rain and were living with no road in, no ferries, and no electricity!

Jo and I had always lived walled up in big cities. For me, it was just a nice trip, but shortly after Jo said, "You know, I would like to live up there." I replied, "No, I don't think so." She said nothing more, just waited me out, letting my imagination work. In time, I would learn to pay careful attention to her ideas.

Dovre at the can buoy in Sea Otter Cove, off Cape Scott, in salmon season.

The village of Quatsino, population one hundred, had thirty-five houses, several empty, scattered along the waterfront on an eleven kilometre stretch of gravel road. Some of the people in Quatsino were happy to see newcomers and wanted us to succeed. They enjoyed watching us struggle and were entertained by our ignorance of the very basics of everyday living. They would laugh, and then graciously show us the way.

Larry Johnson came to our door the second week and said that if I wanted work, he would pick me up every day in his brother's boat, the *Dovre*, a beautiful thirty-two-foot West Coast troller built in 1925. We would go down Neroutsos Inlet to the gyppo logging camp in Atkins Cove, where he was engineer on his family's rented A-frame. He had been so sure I'd say yes that he'd brought me a pair of used cork boots. He said to be at the dock at six in the morning, we would work a ten-hour day, seven days a week, and be back home by six in the evening, weather obliging. When we could not get back, we would bunk with the rest of the crew.

In the morning, I marched down the dock and jumped aboard, walked across the deck to the wheelhouse and stopped dead. Larry was looking at my feet and frowning. I looked down and understood. Then we both looked back at the tracks my cork boots had just punched into the cedar deck. Larry just shook his head.

Setting chokers behind a skidder on a hillside was my first ordeal. Climb the hill with cable and four chokers, set them, run down the hill, ride the skidder to the water, unhook, ride back, climb the hill, set, run down, unhook, ride back, and so forth for ten hours. Like Sisyphus, but why was I being punished?

That first Easter weekend I made more money in four days than I had ever made in a whole month of work—time and a half, and double time for Good Friday and Easter Monday. Almost made me religious.

Next they put me on the A-frame chasing for Larry. It was my task to unhook each log after it came down the mountainside and hit the water. Trouble was I had to walk on floating logs to get to the log I was after. I didn't know how to walk on small second-growth logs. I fell in every day, wet to the waist on cold, windy, snow-in-the-air April days. Finally, I made up my mind to quit if I fell in one more time.

Scrape, scrub, paint and repeat. Photo Tamio Wakayama

The next morning on arrival at the camp, I jumped down with the tie-up line, slipped on a skim of snow, and slid in, as close as I would ever come to a mental breakdown. I figured it out: run, don't walk on small logs, be off and onto the next before the one underfoot can roll and sink.

Each time I had fallen in, I had seen Larry sitting on his machine with his back turned in consideration for my feelings. He didn't want me to see him laughing, but he was carrying my mishaps back to the village for everyone's amusement. Amusement aside, Jo and I worked hard, wanted to learn, and had the requisite endurance.

Just when I was beginning to feel good about logging, Dene Stephenson came to the door and asked if I would work for him at the Quatsino boatyard. I answered, "yes": no more commuting, no more scrambling over match sticks.

Meanwhile, Jo had been quizzing a neighbour about canning and gardening, had taken advice and ordered a canner, cases of cans, a hand crank can sealer and jars, and seeds for the vegetables she was planning to grow. She was also learning to bake bread, which she did for the next thirty years.

Working at the boatyard was a pleasure right from the start. The wooden tugboat *Viner* was on the ways. My first job was to pull off all the protective gum wood, which took my whole first day. The second day, Dene showed me how to reef out all the old soft oakum that was causing the *Viner* to leak. Then Dene spent days working beside me, teaching me to caulk with oakum. Oakum, which is tarred hemp, comes in long bundled strands. It is twisted and punched into the open seams between planks in two layers with the caulking iron, then all set down just right with a making iron. It is then covered with a cement lime mix, nice and smooth, ready for copper paint, tar, a sheet of felt, and beautiful brand-new gumwood overall.

On small boats, the work would be more delicate, cotton and putty rather than oakum and cement. I found I loved caulking seams. The repetition, the narrow focus on the material, the rhythm of the caulking hammer, and the ring of the iron: a bit mindless, maybe, but the skill has been a meal ticket over the years. After the months in the boatyard and the logging, I knew I'd never work inside again. A weight I didn't even know I carried had been lifted.

Dene, a good teacher, explained, directed and demonstrated. I only had to see a thing done once. Even after all these years, when I step up to the bandsaw or pick up a paintbrush, I can hear his voice. "Cut it close," he'd say, and I answered, "How close is close?" "Half a pencil line," he'd say. Or, painting a boot top waterline, "Go fast and you won't have time to make a mistake."

I worked in the boatyard with Dene for two years and never missed a day, learning a bit about everything. Then I bought my first boat. I was ready. A twenty-two-foot B licence troller, the *AnDon*. The former owner helped me rig it and taught me to tie on the gear. The *AnDon* took me through one salmon season and got me a fish patrol with the Department of Fisheries. For the next four years it was summers fishing salmon, then fish patrol in the fall, walking creeks and rivers, counting salmon, reporting problems, and enforcing the Fisheries Act. Then back to the boatyard for the winters, often working with Jack Howich, my next teacher and friend. He also, with his family, took me hunting every fall, and taught me the ethics and rituals of hunting. Jo boned and then canned the whole deer, corned the briskets in ceramic crocks, and sent the hides to Vancouver to be tanned.

When the opportunity came to buy a bigger, A licence troller, I sold the *AnDon* and with a government loan, bought the *Dovre*. But I didn't get a discount for the cork boot damage I had done to the deck three years earlier, which ran from the gunwale to the cabin door. I fished the *Dovre* and did the fish patrol for the next three years, including some frightening storm time out on the Big Water, the Pacific, counting salmon from Brooks Peninsula [Mquqwin] all the way up to the Fisherman River at Cape Scott, plus Quatsino Sound.

There are so many stories to tell about many who didn't survive those years. The closest we came to joining them was on a clear, calm, sunny day. Jo and the dogs aboard, we entered Quatsino Narrows, flying with the incoming tide, staying close to the shore out of the whirlpools. At the far end, there was a cross-current tidal ledge. When we hit, the *Dovre* rolled over onto its starboard side, shifting fuel barrels in the hold and everything on the deck to the downward side. The starboard rail under, Jo and I were thrown against the wheelhouse wall, the whole boat going around in a whirlpool. It happened in an instant. When I turned my head and looked, the water was only a foot from my face, swirling inches from the cabin door. Two more inches and the water would have flooded the wheelhouse; we would have gone straight to the bottom without knowing what had happened to us. I crawled out and up the deck, got the opposite trolling pole down, which lifted us just enough so that I could drive into calm water, anchor, and recover from the shock.

In the off season, I was working around the inlet, beachcombing with the *Dovre*, sawing lumber for people with a portable mill on a float. It was so nice to be home summers after I sold the A salmon licence but kept the C for crabs and prawns.

Jo had insisted on a boat of her own. She would be, she said, like a liberated woman on a bicycle in 1900. We got a sixteen-foot aluminum skiff. I decked over the front third, wedged the bottom at the transom, and raised the twenty-horse outboard until only the cavitation plate and propeller were in the water. When Jo put the engine in gear, the skiff jumped right up onto a plane. It was very fast in good weather and safe in bad. Jo was the only woman in the village who ran her own boat.

At this time, at the boatyard, I built Jo her first table loom. She always knew what she needed and where she was going. She ordered yarn, sat down and began to weave, a book at her side, as if she already knew how. It became a passion and an obsession. She already made much of our clothing; now she was making the cloth as well.

In 1979 Jo said we must leave Quatsino, that we had to go where she could practise her craft. We separated. She spent a short time in Port Hardy, then went to Vancouver. The split made us feel empty and lost. There seemed to be no possible compromise. I understood that she had to go, but I couldn't at first give up the life I was living, although over the next year I did.

After the 1979 herring season, I went to work for Andy Dumyn on the *Arrowac Freighter*, cash buying in Winter Harbour. With the *Dovre*, I towed a log float stacked high with totes of iced sockeye into Winter Harbour from our anchored camp, then towed back with empties. It was a hard summer for the *Dovre* and everyone else. Cocaine, not for pleasure but to drive us, keep us on our feet and awake. Icing fish all night, buying and towing every day, knowing the run could end at any time. But it lasted, a big year for prime, troll-caught sockeye. Maybe it was the last.

When the fish had all gone by or been caught, I sold the *Dovre* to Tomio Wakayama, who had been working with us on the camp, and who

Careta II on a clam digging trip, anchored off Waddington Cove, near Gilford Island.

planned to cruise the coast, doing photography. I sold the sawmill. I put the house up for sale. My heart was not in it any longer. I went to Vancouver and told Jo I did not want to live without her and would join her there. Released from the pain and anxiety, we both wept.

Life in Quatsino had made us, and we just carried on. Jo had built a successful business weaving rugs and yardage for high-end dress makers. I continued doing boat work. We rebuilt a 1909 house to heritage standards and had two more boats.

"I want to learn to sail," Jo said. She took lessons and bought herself a Cal 20. Then when she decided the Cal was too small, she found a derelict up on the hard at Mosquito Creek in North Vancouver. It was the thirty-four-foot sloop *Careta II*, built in 1947. The restoration took us two years, the second year moored at the Maritime Museum as part of the show as we worked.

But the *Careta II* was unhappy in Vancouver, so Jo said, "Why don't we rent the house and explore the coast on the boat?" Eventually, we ended up in Sointula and stayed five years. Next we did what so many North Coast people do: we brought the boat down to the Comox Marina and retired in the Comox Valley. At last, I got to build my own house, and our lives became centred in the arts community.

I am almost at the end of the road now, still heating with wood, still resisting cell phone and email, content with books, the dogs, the birds at the feeder and the Runner ducks in the yard. I keep my caulking and making irons close by on top in my toolbox, to remind me of the many boat bottoms we have caressed over the years.

Jo died in May 2022.

Without Jo, I am just putting in time, waiting it out. The road travelled together turned out to be such a wonder.

Archae and *Grebe*

Hubert Havelaar

More than a century ago, the British writer Kenneth Grahame described the phenomenon perfectly when he wrote "Believe me, my young friend, there is nothing—absolutely nothing—half so much worth doing as simply messing about in boats." My own love of the saltchuck and vessels that manage to stay afloat on it began at an early age. A log raft that I nailed and bolted together and rigged with a burlap square sail was my childhood pride and joy. I'm sure that teredo worms and general decay eventually compromised its flotation, but at the time it kept my feet dry as I explored Portage Inlet, my family's backyard in Victoria. The minimal draught of the raft matched the shallow waters of the inlet and, with a long pole, I could push the contraption to windward. Sufficiently upwind, I would then turn it around and get a glorious downwind run, which admittedly was a lot more fun in a gale. Of course, gale-force winds made the upwind leg a workout, but it was a good lesson: no pain, no gain.

As I got older, that early and modest cruising hinted at potential destinations north up the BC coast, places and undoubtedly adventures I could only dream of. To live the dream probably meant buying a suitably seaworthy boat, but the financial reality that implied was light years from my perennially marginal bank account.

A chance conversation in the spring of 1971 changed everything. Joanne and Illtyd Perkins, who went on to become legendary Gumbooters in Haida Gwaii, excitedly described a twenty-six-foot navy whaleboat hull they had found in Seattle, which they planned to convert into a cruising sailboat. They also mentioned the availability of

Hubert and sons hard at work installing cabin coamings on the *Grebe*.

a sister hull and generously invited my girlfriend and me to tag along and check it out. That second hull was in really rough shape, with cracked ribs and many missing planks, the result of having been used as fenders between large steel navy ships. But I was smitten, and all I could see was the very affordable beginnings of a sailing home on the water. With the characteristic optimism of youth, I embarked on a boatbuilding project.

The timing could not have been better. Boeing, a major economic player in the Seattle area, was struggling and forced to substantially downsize its workforce. The resultant mini-recession meant that many materials were bargain-basement priced, pawn shops were full of cheap but serviceable tools, and our meagre funds stretched a surprisingly long way.

I decided not to repair the decrepit hull with new wood, but instead use its shape as a partial mould and construct a ferro-cement boat with an integral deep keel. The old whaleboat was flipped upside down to make it easier to work on, and sketches were drawn on napkins and the back of envelopes.

Soon, rebar was attached and bent into what I figured a sailing hull should look like. Because it was upside down, it was difficult to view the evolving shape. There was a good deal of bending over double to guide the design, a perspective that was quite disorienting. Ultimately, I could only hope that everything would work out the way I imagined. With the additions of steel mesh, more rebar, sand, cement and some exotic chemicals, something resembling a massive stone whale with a prominent dorsal fin emerged. The hull stayed that way for a month while the concrete cured, and we discretely erected a tent under it. Only a few friends were aware of our under-hull existence and in relative privacy we were entertained by candid comments from complete strangers examining our "sidewalk boat." After launching, the tent was reinstalled inside the open hull and it became our shelter as we were alternately towed and self-propelled home to Victoria.

It was an amazing and foolhardy but grand adventure with an extremely steep learning curve. Flat broke by that time, we resorted to navigating with a roadmap, intuition and a prayer on that first voyage, as we couldn't afford marine charts. We were young and felt immortal, but when we struck an offshore reef that the roadmap didn't show and the hull started taking on water, we proved that some substitutions could be downright dangerous. We survived, persevered, got jobs and quickly constructed decks, cabin and a rudimentary interior that made moving aboard possible. It was rustic, crude even, but it was a start. I named our new floating home *Archae*, Greek for "the beginning" and root for words like archaeology. With oil-finished woodwork, hand-stitched recycled cotton sails and wood smoke curling from the stovepipe, the boat looked as archaic as the name suggested.

Best of all, *Archae* became our ticket to explore the coast and meet dozens of kindred spirits on boats and from communities between the Gulf Islands and the Broughton Archipelago. Even though our accommodations were tight for two adults, we managed to squeeze a cat and dog aboard as well. Eventually, our first son's arrival persuaded us that it was time to move ashore or build a larger boat.

Archae cruising in the Salish Sea.

We did both, on a piece of raw land on Denman Island where my parents planned to retire in four years' time. Those full-on years flew by in a blur of parenting and constructing a house, workshop, boatshed and boat, with a smattering of local paid work to keep the proverbial wolf from the door. The boat, a sixteen-tonne version of a British pilot cutter that I sized to accommodate a family of four, was lofted the week after our second son's arrival. I built it fairly traditionally, with a Douglas fir backbone, oak frames (ribs), and epoxy-sheathed red cedar strip planking. I was able to do most of the boatbuilding on my own, but many friends showed up at critical times to give me much appreciated help, which was so typical of the boating community we were so lucky to be part of.

Launching day became a spontaneous regatta as Baynes Sound filled with a spectacular variety and number of boats and their crews, welcoming the *Grebe* to its natural element. Adding to the water-borne festivities, a friend, who really wanted to be there but was working with Search and Rescue out of Comox that day, made several heart-stopping low passes over the fleet with the spotter plane, and later returned to hover directly overhead in the twin-rotor Labrador chopper. That evening, we laid out an enormous potluck dinner in the now boatless shed, and an impromptu band of musical friends entertained us. It was quite a celebration.

The sailing rig would have to come later, but we were excited to be

The *Grebe* under full canvas in Desolation Sound.

on the water and mobile again. Our inaugural crossing of the Strait of Georgia on the *Grebe* was memorable. We set off across the Comox bar in a fifteen-knot westerly and I was thrilled with how the boat, powered by a brand new Sabb diesel, handled the waves. It felt unstoppable, right up until the engine faltered and suddenly quit. Typically for westerlies, the wind had increased in the afternoon and, now dead in the water, the boat turned broadside to the lumpy waves. With no mast and rigging to counteract the substantial weight of the ballast keel, the vessel became a nautical metronome and rolled like a drunk pig. That dreadful motion combined with the reek of raw diesel spilt during my frantic mechanical investigations resulted in a green-hued and unhappy crew. I recall looking over to mountainous Texada Island and wondering if I had made a terrible mistake building a new home on the water. Fortunately, wonderful friends who were accompanying us in their boat saved the day by towing us to safety. In the blessedly calm water in the lee of Savary Island, I managed to figure out what had caused the breakdown. It seems that my preschool kids, while "helping" their dad sweep the decks during construction had discovered and unscrewed the bronze filler plates engraved with the word DIESEL and found a nifty place to empty handfuls of sawdust. That material made a remarkably effective fuel line logjam. After a lot of flushing and filtering, the fuel resumed making its way to the engine and that trusty engine never failed us again.

Cortes Island became home base, an easy choice with its wonderful community, numerous public and private wharves, and docks for access, schools for the boys, all within spitting distance of Desolation Sound, a world-class cruising destination. In addition, the extensive Salish Sea to the south and the rapids and channels north provided all the spectacular and adventurous cruising we could possibly want.

Eventually we sold the *Grebe* to pay for land and a home ashore. *Kyra,* a twenty-three-foot cat-rigged sloop and, later, a classic plastic thirty-five-foot sloop, *Osprey,* satisfied our need to stay engaged with the saltchuck. My childhood dreaming evolved and stretched into more than sixty years of "simply messing about with boats": navigating channels, rounding capes, crossing straits, heading up inlets and anchoring in idyllic coves to walk on remote beaches. Inevitably, the years have passed, many friends and their boats have moved on, and relationships have shifted, but the soul-enriching summers afloat are constant and remain a priority for us. We often look out at *Osprey* swinging patiently on the mooring and realize how incredibly fortunate we are that more saltwater adventures are just a sail-raising away.

Arrawac Freighter and Baidarka

Joe Ziner

Ever since I was a Boy Scout, I'd known the real forests were in the North-west. In February 1969, I headed west on the train from Montreal. I was seventeen.

I stayed at a house in Burnaby, where I had friends who were students at Simon Fraser University. It felt really great to be in the west. That summer I hitched back east and made it down to the Woodstock Music Festival with friends. What a great trip! My generation's culture was strong, but it was not for me. I'd had a taste of the west coast of Vancouver Island and that now felt like home.

Red snapper caught with an Air Canada spoon lure. Photo D.M. Holyoke

I signed up for the fall and winter terms at the Vancouver Art School. During my first year, I was inconveniently living in Haney, about an hour's drive east up the Fraser Valley. In 1970, must have been April as there were apple blossoms, my housemate had a visit from a political radical from Toronto. He was keen to meet certain people but did not drive. I had just got my licence and we borrowed a car. We went to the Maplewood Mud Flats and met Paul Spong, a neuroscientist who was very interested in making meaningful contact with whales. He soon established OrcaLab on Hanson Island, where he has now been for fifty years.

Then we went to meet Ken Drushka and Brian Lewis,

Joe Ziner drawing

who were gearing up for a cedar salvaging operation on East Thurlow Island. Buckets of axe handles, sacks of flour, talk of giant windfall cedar, boats and tides. They called the project Cosmic Logging, and it was a state of mind, not a business plan. I could tell it was something I wanted to be a part of, and my art background was welcome. They had put an ad in the *Georgia Straight*: "Wanted, Cosmic Loggers, make 0-35$ per day 100 miles North of Vancouver. Either you're a Cosmic Logger or you're not. *Ingrid*, C float False Creek." Clearly, we needed to screen all of the people that were going to answer that ad. I made up a set of Rorschach ink blot prints and, with a straight face, listened to their impressions. Very interesting. Of course, there was no judgment, everyone who wanted to cooperate came along.

Ken and Brian were very resourceful. Brian had traded the leaky old *Ingrid* for a panel truck, which we towed up to the island on a float. Ken especially loved to "mount an operation" and it was he who knew how to work cedar and held the Minor Forest Products lease that was the legal basis of our residency on Crown Land. I cut cedar and explored the land and sea that summer.

Come September, I thought I could do both the work in the woods and art school, but I needed special permission for the second year. I went to see the venerable principal, Fred Amess, in his office, and told him that I was proud to be a student, but I was drawn to the upcoast world of cedar. Was there a way I could combine them? With his blessing it was back to Thurlow Island for the year, which included my first winter in the bush. I had my camera and documented projects and places, which I presented as a slide show to the instructors in the spring. That's how I got through art school and entrenched myself in a remote forest at the same time.

For the next four years there was no other industrial or private activity on the island. Ken applied for the Opportunities for Youth employment grants that brought new people in the summer for watershed surveys and other work.

I loved the life of a young woodsman and somehow was able to spend several unhindered summers and winters there. I thought and felt that

The *Arrawac Freighter* with a load of herring has settled onto its marks. I'd zoomed off in the skiff to take the photo and the skipper is hollering at me.

I became part of the landscape and the seasons, living out in the air and making my world out of cedar and twine. We made most things out of clear split cedar. I inherited the use of the *Nodales Queen*, a sixteen-foot Turner Boatworks skiff, carvel-planked cedar on oak, which needed work. I made a rickety grid in Thurston Bay and sistered the frames with flattened and soaked cedar boughs. I bent and clench nailed them. For power, it had a Seagull Century, 102cc outboard motor with a clutch. It had a carved cedar gas cap and various repairs had been done with fishing line and epoxy. Its elemental nature was to run, and it could always be fixed.

One spring day down at Camp O Bay, we met a boat that had come with supplies. The skipper, Andy Dumyn, said, "Hey Ziner, want to go fishing?" Indeed, I did, and he nosed the bowsprit up to the rocks and I gumbooted aboard the *Gondola*, a fifty-foot 1905 cod boat, and for the first time stood a wheel watch as we steered up Johnstone Strait and eventually around

Cape Scott to Winter Harbour. We jigged cod and snapper off Cape Cook with some hungry locals, their boats periodically disappearing in the troughs of the waves, then bravely popping up on the crests. I remember handing over my only twenty-dollar bill for fuel in Kyuquot. That boat went on to other adventures after that, but all without my help.

After a while, Andy found an incredible boat to run, and I was offered work on it. I was now a deckhand on a packer called the *Arrawac Freighter*, a beautiful sixty-five-foot ship. Built in Vancouver in 1891 as the *Beatrice*, it was certainly one of the oldest of the West Coast's working boats. It started its career as a sealing schooner, but soon was fitted with the first of two steam engines and worked as a tug. In 1962, it was fitted with an 8L3 Gardner, which was awesome. I worked on the boat from 1974 for four or five years, heading to other haunts in winter and between fisheries, but if the boat went anywhere, I was usually on it.

Sitting on the beach, Hot Spring Cove, in Clayoquot Sound not too far from Tofino. It was the beginning of a gillnet herring trip, not the end. In that sense, it had a formality about it as captured by Joe's posture. We, fishermen and women, such as me, the lot of us, are sensitive to beginnings and ending of voyages. In retrospect, this was a ritualistic bathing—a getting clean before beginning the hard work of being on the ocean in the winter, looking for fish that may or may not be there in competition with others struggling to do the same. So, there we are at Hot Spring Cove, the *Arrawac Freighter* crew, all ready for whatever comes next. Photo Tamio Wakayama

I always had paper and ink in my kit. If I had time, I'd make a sketch or a direct fish print. The wild and grand environment and the imperative nature of commercial fishing evokes epic drama, but there was never time for a careful study. It was enough to try to capture something of the time and place.

In February we'd outfit for the herring fishery, which at that time was for all of March. We would progress northward, following the last of winter, week by week. When the season closed and we'd head south, spring would come on extra strong. More refit, much scraping and painting of the boat and barge down in Ladner, followed by cash buying salmon at Winter Harbour and ice packing for the thirty-six-hour run to Vancouver, turn-around every week from about the first of May. We could pack 65,000 pounds of fish and ice. The life suited my bachelor status. I would often take a night shift at the wheel, which necessitated keeping track of all lights.

> moving at midnight out from Winter Harbour
> full moon and light swells
> gillnets sprinkling the horizon with lights
> steering boat all night
> May moon rounding Cape Scott
> guided by radar smack centred on
> Cassiopeia under which hang electric curtains
> passed over Nahwitty Bar, first light of a clear
> morning; moonset; stars bright; east
> light; shooting stars; jet trail white;
> flat calm phosphorescence about
> bow and sides; even orange pulse of
> radar; silent frenetic blinking of sounder;
> cigarette glow; channel markers real and imagined

In 1977, I was twenty-five and, after my third herring season, I joined George Dyson on a baidarka expedition to south-east Alaska and back which took most of the year. George had a plan to repopulate the coast with big sailing kayaks and asked me to join in his enterprise. He'd been building and testing designs, evolved from the Aleut baidarka, for six years. I was confident in the boats and George's ideas. I was all in, for the build, the trips and the histories, old and new.

These 1977 boats, of which we built six, were twenty-eight-foot, three-hatch sea kayaks, designed for sustained travel on the outer coasts. They are

Baidarka VI, flying down Clarence Strait, Alaska, on the afternoon northwest wind, 1977. Photo G.B. Dyson

an engineering marvel, with tensile fibreglass skin around the compressive frame. The frames and stringers are formed aluminum tubes lashed with nylon cordage, and the bow and stern assemblies integrate the stringers with plate, all drilled and lashed together. To get the skin so thin and tight, the frame is first covered in cellophane that is shrunk to fit. This supports the fibreglass cloth and minimizes the resin. With the spruce floorboards they weighed 150 pounds. This has all been beautifully documented in George's book, *Baidarka.*

With a big vessel, a considered approach is predictable and efficient. This was also the sensibility with these large kayaks: they made you think ahead. Two people per boat was optimal capacity, what was essential was unity of intent. Donna Holyoke and I paddled out from Gustavus, our base camp, toward the outer coast. We rode the ebb tide like a river out the North Inian Pass and into Taylor Bay. We found ourselves a tiny bit of beach on an island and set up the tent between some salmonberries, but we had to move it from there when a tuft of fur alerted me that this was the bear's path. There were fresh tracks there in the morning. A close call, but I made a paintbrush from that tuft and painted eyes on the boat, which helped it come to life.

The intent of the expedition was to push north. We wanted northern drama, to be part of something truly wild. Lituya Bay was an intriguing goal. Once you have rounded Cape Spencer from Cross Sound, the most northerly inlet of Alaska's Alexander Archipelago, it is the Gulf of Alaska all the way out. For thirty miles up to Icy Point there are some interesting bays and a great stone arch that we rode through on a wave. Past Icy Point, the La Perouse Glacier snakes down from the Fairweather Range to tidewater and there is no safe break in the shoreline for twenty nautical miles until the narrow entrance to Lituya Bay, safest to be crossed only at slack water on a good day. To get to Lituya Bay became a reachable goal from Icy Point. The Macy brothers in *Baidarka VI* agreed to meet us there, making their own paddling plan.

George and I paddled our boat the twenty nautical miles through one twilit night. I remember the sounds and smells of the sea lions outside the bay in the dark. The early dawn revealed a scene of geological trauma on a grand scale that was the result of a quake in 1958, which triggered a massive slide at the head of the bay, forming a wave that stripped the forests from the sidehills over five hundred metres and swept anchored fishboats out over the spit at the entrance. The beaches are still stacked with silvered trees with roots and is patrolled by brown bears. It was a very awesome place and not a restful camp situation, but it was as north and as wild as we could get, and I was satisfied. It was a memorable place to turn our expedition around.

It took several days of tailwinds and fair tides to get back to the settlement of Gustavus for July fourth festivities, which included kayak races up the Good River and American food. The other four boats had their own plans for further adventures, but George and I elected to run our two boats south, a pull for home that took weeks. Sometimes, with a strong northwest wind behind, we'd make great time through those Alaskan waters. In that year I was six months living on the water with the baidarka.

The following year, 1978, I made a trip to the Brooks Peninsula [Mquqwin], out of Quatsino Sound. My companion was the Danish ornithologist, Dr. Niels Krabbe, who had a notion to add the albatross to his life list. That they mostly stayed well out at sea was not a deterrent; we'd get close anyway. We crossed Brooks Bay and were heading for a remote creek mouth with sand bars. There was a bit of ground swell and we surfed into the creek mouth. Incongruously, there appeared two guys in ski jackets, biologists from the University of British Columbia, moss-men, and we soon shared their camp. The Brooks Peninsula had not been glaciated and, with unique plants, held special interest. My ornithologist knew a fair bit about the subject, and they traded botanical insights, peppered with Latin, around the fire.

*

It looked like the 1979 herring season was going to be big. By this time, I had married my baidarka paddling companion, Donna, and we had just had a baby. It was good timing to make some money, though it meant going to sea for a month. With only two or three seasoned fishermen available, the skipper took a free hand in hiring on his friends for crew. There was Moe, a dairy farmer; Jeff, a city bus driver; Brian Lewis, our most experienced mariner; Tamio Wakayama, an artist/photographer on adventure; me, deckhand/artist; and Andy, our skipper, a careful gambler. I would say the crew was diverse but united in intent to catch fish. Certainly, we were better equipped than in previous years. Still, there was some downtime, waiting.

> Lousy weather, premature fish,
> excess of boats, cost/time erratic.
> Only the seagulls seem to profit,
> low overhead.

The herring were abundant at times that season, and the prices rose by the hour. Three years before, each herring shaken into the boat was worth a nickel, now they were quarters and would go higher. The price per tonne was $2,500 to $3,000. Soon we moved in the right direction and found a quiet lagoon filled with herring with nobody around. We were on top of the schools with two nets, within hailing distance of the boat. Of course, our lights were out. Under a dull moon with flat, protected but open water, nets were generously catching fish. With good catches, prices up, and a teriyaki dinner, everybody aboard was feeling pretty good.

It was a brief time of gold rush mentality, which included seeing the "Million Dollar Set" at Burnaby Narrows and our own full cargo nets. For me, fishing had been a trade, and the work was a craft, not an industrial assault. I was impressed with the gow ponds of Haida Gwaii. They produced herring roe on kelp, a traditional food, where the netted fish would be slowly towed into pens to spawn on hung kelp and afterwards released. Here was a lesson in sustainability to be learned at the height of a roe herring fishing season.

I lost heart in the fishery and, after that, gave myself over to family life and carpentry work, which soon involved a boat of our own and another chapter on the water.

Atarax, Native Girl and Tuya

Dane Campbell

Being born in Saskatchewan and growing up in the foothills of southern Alberta do not explain my love for the ocean. The same can be said of my two younger brothers, who have sixty-five years combined experience with boats on the BC coast.

I was fifteen years old when we first arrived on Vancouver Island and rented a house near Sidney, on the water's edge. I immediately started to build an eight-foot sailing pram called a Sabot. The Slegg brothers had their first store in Sidney and were a great help in selecting materials. With advice and help from others, soon I was free, sailing the Sabot around Shoal Bay Harbour.

My friends Barry Matthews, Fred Molten and I were always hanging about boats. Around the time I was seventeen, Barry created a plywood barge, powered by a huge gas engine, with a pusher air prop, which raced over the water at a great speed. We decided to brew beer on Little Shell Island, with an oil lantern for heat under a cardboard box. Daily trips to the island kept us busy stirring the brew and filling the oil lantern. After a week, the brew was ready for bottling, the summer weather was perfect and there was a lamb barbecue on Saturna Island, so off we headed in the flying barge. We camped on the beach, enjoying the barbecue and fresh new beer. Then we heard the Job's Daughters organization for

Aboard *Tuya* with son Adam on my knee.

young women was having a dance at the community hall. We hiked over to the hall, but uninvited guests were not allowed in.

In 1960, the new BC Ferries had just started running from Swartz Bay to Tsawwassen. For a hoot, we boarded the ferry and bought a bus ticket to Vancouver. We had heard the movie theatres ran all night. Not having anywhere to stay or much cash, we thought we could sleep in the theater. But at midnight they booted us out, so we headed to some grassy land by the bus depot to sleep under some newspapers. By morning, the sun woke us up and we found ourselves surrounded by other wayward folk, snoring away. After a cheap breakfast, we caught a bus back to the ferry. So much for the bright lights of Vancouver.

Between finishing high school and developing a photography business I continued to dream about boats. During the summer I worked on several fish packers owned by Tulloch Western Fisheries in Vancouver. With these earnings my friend Paul Stenner and I planned a trip around the world, first via P&O Liners to Hawaii, Fiji, New Zealand and Australia. Next, I flew to the Solomon Islands to work for Inco, a Canadian-owned mining company, for four months. Back in Sydney, Australia, Paul's friend arranged for me to work on an oil tanker, the *Oscar Gordon*, through Indonesia and the Suez Canal. We were away from Canada for a year and a half.

Upon returning I spent two years at the University of Victoria during which I longed to further explore the BC coast. I built a seventeen-foot kayak and circumnavigated Vancouver Island in ten weeks one summer. That fall I sailed to San Francisco on a trimaran called *Highlight* with the two Glennie brothers from New Zealand. After this voyage, I dreamed of visiting the Queen Charlotte Islands [Haida Gwaii]. I fell in love with a twenty-six-foot gaff-rigged cutter, *Atarax*, in the Inner Harbour of Victoria. This vessel changed my life as I fulfilled my dream of visiting the Charlottes and met Helen Piddington, who became my wife for fifty-four years.

We soon realized we needed more space for serious cruising and Allen and Sharie Farrell agreed to sell us the *Native Girl*, their thirty-nine-foot ketch. Soon, we were headed back to the Charlottes in *Native Girl* when John A. MacDonald, the Fisheries officer for the Northern Coast, offered us a position. We were hired as fisheries guardians on Princess Royal Island in Laredo Inlet for four seasons, an ideal job for us. By this time, we had a beautiful daughter aboard. As we were cruising, we were looking to find a place to settle, a property with a wharf.

My plans of sailing the South Pacific were fading and by 1974 we moved into an old log house on a property in Sidney Bay, Loughborough

Helen and I at the Queen Charlotte City (Daajing Giids) dock on board *At-arax*.

Inlet. Homesteading soon took over sailing and *Native Girl* became our freight boat, moving all our possessions from Horseshoe Bay to Sidney Bay. *Native Girl* held a commercial licence because it had been built with a live tank amidships for cod fishing. In those days, a ten-dollar commercial licence allowed most species to be fished year-round. I started prawn fishing to bring in much-needed income. My first traps were hand-built cedar box traps, hand hauled over the edge of our rubber inflatable Canova. I hand hauled up to twelve traps at a time and I could freeze the prawns in an old kerosene deep freezer.

After four years, Allen Farrell wanted to buy *Native Girl* back, so I had to find another boat. I went to Sidney and while sailing past the Swartz Bay ferry terminal, an interesting-looking vessel caught my eye. I told myself that was the kind of boat that I would like to own. As fortune would have it, the vessel was for sale and within two days I was the owner of the *Tuya*, which had been built at Benson's Shipyard in Vancouver.

Soon, I was catching crab for local restaurants and lodges. Eventually, I bought a twenty-one-foot aluminum herring skiff, the *Yellow Fellow*, and installed a Briggs & Stratten drum puller. It was not the safest of boats, but it was fast. Occasionally, we would have to turn around on a supply run to Kelsey Bay because of bad weather. One time, we were returning from

Campbell River in *Yellow Fellow* late at night and arrived at the mouth of the Inlet in pitch darkness. It was so dark we could not even see the skyline of the mountains. We followed the shore up the east side of the Inlet and before long I realized it was actually the west side. We had completely circled to port and were heading away from our destination. Turning around, we eventually made home port without mishap.

Yellow Fellow improved prawning production and in 1985 we decided to ask Steve Daigle to build us a twenty-four-foot high-speed boat which we named *Kitasu*. This proved a right move as about the same time the Department of Fisheries started changing the regulation by limiting licences and shortening

Tuya on our grid in Sidney Bay with dog Cedar, a ridgeback from Swanson Island.

the season, which escalated the value of the fisheries. I ended up with two prawn licences, and I decided to trade one for a Hitachi backhoe to help work our woodlot. At the time I was offered a job booming for McLean Logging in Beaver Inlet and then for Ted Leroy Trucking across the Inlet. Once, when the outboard on the rubber inflatable stopped working, I had to rely on my fourteen-foot Madill boom boat to travel two miles across the Inlet. Helen was always concerned that I would make the crossing safely and she'd follow my progress with binoculars to make sure I made it and didn't sink mid-channel.

Once the booming ended and the logging camp left, I got really serious about crab and prawn fishing, now that I had the new boat. The regulations were changing and, in order to keep both fisheries on *Kitasu*, we had to go to a Fisheries Review Panel and face an appeal board in Vancouver. The crab licence did not have the sufficient record of sales to meet the new regulations, but the review panel was sympathetic to my appeal as I had just invested in the new high-speed fishboat, and they allowed both licences to be married. As fishing pressure increased for prawns, the season soon went from year-round to one or two months. Crab fishing is now a one-a-week pull in order to manage the fishery.

Over the years I have owned fourteen vessels that have helped fill the needs of coastal living. The only other way to reach our property is by sea-plane or helicopter, which we could not afford to use. I have worked on ten deep-sea ships and travelled on many others.

Nowadays, I rely on my thirty-foot EagleCraft cruiser, *Silver Loon*, for commuting to town and packing supplies. When the weather is pleasant, I can still put in a day's work but at a much slower pace. My son is eager to take over the responsibilities of owning this coastal property. I am so pleased to let his capable hands continue improving life in the Inlet. My daughter is tied as much to the sea and the land on Gabriola as she was growing up in Sidney Bay. If the future allows, with the help of my partner, Maggie, and new knee joints, I hope to have many more years in this blessed place.

Bamberton

Brian Lewis

In mid-June 1959, two months short of my seventeenth birthday, I climbed out of a float plane with a duffle bag at the Good Hope Cannery in Rivers Inlet. My father, Ed, had asked his friend Norm to find me a summer job in the fishing industry. Norm could say yes because he managed a number of coastal, commercial fishing camps owned by the ABC Packing Company.

I walked up a ramp to a large timbered dock where I could look down at a boat about sixty-five-feet long, with the name *Silver Bear* painted on the bow. Tied alongside was a fishboat, with a fisherman standing on deck tossing fresh salmon into an aluminum bucket on the deck of the *Silver Bear*. Once the bucket was full, a deckhand weighed the contents before opening a gate at the front of the bucket and letting the fish spill down into a cargo hold where a young man about my age with a cigarette in his mouth began shovelling ice onto the fish. All the while, the smell of fresh coffee wafted up from somewhere aboard. Seeing all this for the first time: the boats, fisherman, workers, ice, coffee and sea, I could not have told you where I was on a map, but I knew beyond a shadow of a doubt that wherever this place

Hotspring Island, Haida Gwaii.

was, it was the right place. That was all that mattered. "But wait," I said to myself, "I'm not here to sling fish or shovel ice. I'm here to be the assistant bookkeeper."

So it was that later the same day I found myself at a desk in a neat, freshly painted office, copying numbers from green slips of papers into a large, hardcover accounting ledger that took two hands to open and close. It took Wally, the long-suffering bookkeeper, exactly twelve excruciating days before he fired me for doing a bad job, and for spending countless unauthorized hours away from my desk helping fishermen with their boats. Norm flew up from Alert Bay to deal with the situation. Instead of firing me as I feared, he told me to keep scrubbing out fish holds or doing whatever it was fishermen required. I was no longer the assistant bookkeeper; I was now known around camp as the "dock assistant." Wally didn't seem to mind my sticking around now that I was out of his hair, and I felt the same about him and his two-fisted ledger.

Good Hope Cannery was a hub of fishing activity, though no actual canning happened there anymore. Fishermen could deliver their catch, have a shower, do laundry, buy groceries, and most importantly, talk to each other... a lot. Regardless of how short or long a conversation, it was never over until one of the parties volunteered what a shame it was there were no fish around, anywhere. This was interesting because, likely as not, the speaker was one of those who as recently as last week had nearly sunk his boat by overloading it with premium sockeye salmon. It was with these people, in this world, that I spent the rest of the summer, happy as a clam. Reluctantly, in early September I left Good Hope for Vancouver, home and school.

In the spring of the next year, 1960, Norm hired me back, not as a dock assistant and not at Good Hope, but as a real, honest-to-goodness deckhand on a forty-foot fish collector called *Margan*, working out of Alert Bay. I was determined to be the best deckhand ever built. I steered the boat, weighed the fish, shovelled the ice and scrubbed the decks until they shone. I learned to splice, tie a bowline and dress out salmon like a pro. I loved the work. Eventually, Labour Day rolled around and, like the previous year, I hitched a ride on a fish packer back to Vancouver, this time to register for classes at the University of British Columbia.

The next year, 1961, something really big happened. Norm made me skipper of my own boat, *Madelon*. It was forty-two feet long, narrow, deep and could hold about ten tonnes of iced fish. My deckhand, Richard, was the boyfriend of Norm's younger daughter Norma. Richard was a tall, low-key, pleasant fellow, a year younger than me and a good, steady worker. I wouldn't call us friends, but we worked well together: he slow and steadfast, me fast and eager. Day after day, in any weather, *Madelon* collected more fish from fishermen than any similar boat working Johnstone Strait between Blinkhorn Light and the Broken Islands.

One August evening, Norm told me he wanted me to leave the next morning to locate and collect fish from a group of gillnetters rumoured to be fishing about four hours west of Alert Bay around the Port Hardy Airport. This would be new country for me. We left at first light and headed west past Port McNeill and, by about 10 o'clock, we were off the Airport on a sunny morning, flat calm with not a fishboat in sight, but the day was young, so we continued west hoping to find the illusive fleet.

By noon we had reached the entrance to Hardy Bay and still no boats. I had to decide whether to turn back toward Alert Bay or keep going up Goletas Channel. It was a sunny afternoon with a light westerly wind and the chart promised interesting new places with names like Scarlett Point, God's Pocket, Nigei Island, Shushartie Bay and Bull Harbour. Full of youthful curiosity, I made the decision to keep going west along Goletas Channel. It was about an hour later when I first began to feel the westerly swells getting larger and decided they were nothing *Madelon* couldn't handle. Richard was down below in the galley preparing sandwiches when, all of a sudden, *Madelon* started to pitch wildly in a series of short steep waves, which came out of nowhere. I eased back on the throttle. Soon, green water was flooding over the bows onto the foredeck. Heavy spray covered the windscreen, making visibility impossible. The wheelhouse door that was notoriously difficult to slide open was now going back and forth like greased lightning. Books began to fly off the wheelhouse shelf and then my binoculars flew by my head before slamming into a far bulkhead. Just then, Richard's head appeared from the galley below and looking up at me he shouted, "Where the hell are we?" All I could do was stare down at him and shout back, "I don't know!" all the while standing spread legged while gripping the steering wheel and doing my best to keep *Madelon* pointed into the onslaught. Finally, sensing the boat had reached the bottom of a trough, I jammed the throttle full ahead and spun the steering wheel hard to port. The boat crawled up the next wave and at the same time heeled farther and farther to port until the side deck was awash and *Madelon* was on the verge of capsizing. It lay there a long moment as if deciding whether to just give up the struggle and roll over or try to sit up straight and carry on. It was touch and go until *Madelon* came around nearly 120 degrees and the side deck water began to drain away through the many freeing ports on that side. Slowly, ever so slowly, it righted itself until, finally, I allowed myself to believe we might survive after all. By now, we had turned through 180 degrees and were facing due east in the direction of Alert Bay. When I was sure Richard was okay, I had him steer slowly down Goletas Channel while I checked the bilges, hatch covers, fish hold and foredeck for flooding or damage. All was as it should be, except the exterior decks and wheelhouse windows were mysteriously peppered with fine white sand. I had no idea how the sand got there until I located my mariner's handbook on the wheelhouse floor and read about the area. I realized I had unthinkingly tried to pass over the infamous Nahwitti Bar on a falling tide with an opposing westerly wind pushing large swells from the open Pacific down Goletas Channel. I understood that severe turbulence had swept sand off the shallow bottom to the surface before flinging it at us with every wave we encountered. There was no denying what had happened. I had failed to pay attention to what was going on around me with near catastrophic consequences. By forgetting to check where we were, I had come close to ending our lives.

With that sobering realization now swirling around in my nineteen-year-old brain, I was glad of the distraction of having to do something about the disaster that was the galley. Floor to deckhead was an unholy spectacle of ketchup, mixed with rice, baking soda, pancake syrup, cereal, cheese slices, juice, milk and broken dishes, all of which, in the space of a few harrowing minutes, had flown off shelves, out of cupboards and out of the fridge as *Madelon* tumbled in the confused sea. Somehow, a bag of pancake mix had broken open on my bunk.

Eventually, with a fresh cup of coffee in one hand and a smoke in the other, I opened the throttle and made steady eight-knot headway toward Alert Bay, arriving there well after dark with not one fish aboard to justify having been gone so long and so far. For me, something profound had taken place that made that the trip of a lifetime. The next day and every day after that, I remained the high energy, workaholic kid who aimed to be the best damned skipper that ever lived. But that egocentric goal was now tempered by a new and profound respect for the awesome power of the sea. I learned that, unless I was constantly mindful of where I was on the water and the sea around me, I was risking my life and that of anyone under my care and command. As it turned out, the lesson I learned at the Nahwitti Bar on that sunny afternoon way back in 1961 has needed many refresher courses over the years.

In 1974, I owned the troller *Bamberton* and fished between the Brooks Peninsula [Mquqwin] and Kains Island on the west coast of Vancouver Island. Playing forward the Nahwitti Bar lesson, I learned to plot courses as a safety tool to supplement local knowledge. One moonlit night in July, I had fished late and was returning from sea to Quatsino Sound. With my chart beside me, I hunched over the compass light, doggedly steering the home-ward course I had plotted that afternoon. About fifteen minutes into the thirty-five-minute run, my eye was drawn to unexpected movement directly outside the open starboard wheelhouse door. There, close enough to touch and lit by the light of the moon, was white water cascading off giant rocks momentarily exposed by the retreating ground swell. I was unfazed, saying to myself, "I plotted the course; I did it correctly and I'm safe following it." Such arrogance!

It wasn't until a few years later when I attended navigation courses at the Marine Institute in Vancouver that I realized my plot failed to include the essential elements of variation and deviation and was therefore useless and dangerous. Looking back, my safe passage that night was a mix of good intention, mangled procedure and gobs of luck. I keep on learning. Rock on.

Broughton I

Kit Eakle

I came to visit friends on Malcolm Island in the summer of 1969, staying at their homestead for a week with my wife. It was magical, and we decided to return after my graduation from the University of California that December. My wife had meanwhile become pregnant, and the draft lottery in the US had determined that I was number six out of three hundred and sixty-five in priority for the draft after graduation. The friends with the homestead were going to spend a year in China, so they asked us to look after their place in Sointula. Jumping at the chance, in March of 1970, I packed all our worldly goods in the back of our GMC panel van, headed north, and immigrated to Canada.

The friends' homestead was eight kilometres out a dirt road from the small Finnish settlement of Sointula, established in the early 1900s by Finnish anarchist miners who had worked the coal mines in Cumberland and Nanaimo on Vancouver Island. The Finns started Sointula as communal utopia on Malcolm Island, off the northeast coast of Vancouver Island. That community had long before broken up into small family farms, and with the coming of electricity, many moved into the little town and supported themselves largely from salmon fishing.

In the spring of 1970, we joined the beginnings of a nascent cultural clash of incoming hippies living alongside Finnish fishermen

On the Sointula dock with Sointula fisher Charlie Peterson on the left.

who had no idea what to make of the young outsiders suddenly invading their insular and long-established island community. For us "invaders," finding some means of financial support was crucial, especially for me with a brand new daughter delivered at home in July 1970.

A few of the younger residents on the island became friends with us strange outsiders, eager for contact with intriguingly "worldly" folks from distant places. One such person was Billy Clegg. Billy had the blond look of the Finns, and informed me one day that his boat captain, Jimmy Tarkanen, a scion of one of the original Finnish settler families, was looking for another crew member for his table seiner, the *Broughton I.*

No other outsider had yet broken into the Sointula fishing fleet as a crew member. And I knew that the fishermen of that time often made small fortunes, sometimes in one opening, which lasted for only two to four days of

Jim Tarkanen's table seiner, *Broughton I,* piling net on the table or deck.

fishing. I jumped at the chance, knowing I was breaking through some sort of unwritten barrier, and was not necessarily welcomed by all.

The first opening on the fishing grounds of Blackfish Sound, south of Malcolm Island, was buzzing with boats lining up, vying for position with the smaller gillnetters along the channel. Large seine boats also lined up.

By 1970 most seine boats were "drum seiners," with a large steel drum mounted on the back, powered by a motor that allowed the net to be pulled in quickly and efficiently once a set was made. With the fish encircled the weighted lead line is drawn up and the rings between the lead weights are hung on the large brass "hairpin" pursing the net so no fish bigger than the net mesh can escape. The drum reels the cork in and the lead-line back onto the drum until the fish are brought alongside the boat. If the catch is too large to drag over the stern, a brailing net is used to brail the fish fifty or so at a time into the boat's hold.

Unlike a drum seiner, the *Broughton I*, one of the last working table seiners on the coast, had to tie its net to the shore on a permanently installed steel stake embedded in the rocks at a strategic point.

Both drum seiners and table seiners require a large skiff that hangs off the end of the net. Drum seiners might also have an engine-powered skiff to hold the net behind the seine boat as it makes its set. The skiff then delivers the ends of the lead and float line to crew members on the larger boat, tying up in the case of the drum seiner and joining the crew in guiding the corks, leads and net to the proper sides of the drum.

In the case of the table seiner, the net is drawn in by a small, powered block hanging off the rigging over the back deck or table of the boat. In this scenario the net comes in *much* slower than on the drum seine. Because the cork line can drift around the boat, the table seiner works much better if the end of the net is fixed on the shore, hence the need for tying the net to the permanent stakes on the rocky shore. That also means instead of one skiff man to manage the boat, another man is needed to tie the net to shore while the other manages the skiff. Eventually, the seiner comes around and calls the two men back. The skiff man rows to the boat as quickly as possible, and the shore man jumps on the big boat with the lead line, allowing the pursing of the net. He then joins the crew on board. Three men are required, one each to pile the lead line, the net, and the cork line on the deck and keep the lines from tangling.

Meanwhile, the skiff man does the grunt work pulling the cork line as hard and fast as possible and piling the corks and line into the skiff to keep the bag formed by the floating cork line from drifting around the stern of the boat and getting fouled in the propeller of the seiner. That was my job. I never imagined that the weight and pull of the long line of small, white football-shaped corks floating on the ocean surface would be so great. Each hard pull yielded a yard or so of rope as I piled the line and floats into the bobbing skiff while the crew on board, clearly impatient with the greenhorn in the skiff, yelled, "Pull! Pull harder!"

That first overcast afternoon it also started raining mid-set. All around us, drum seiners set quickly in the open ocean. Trollers and gillnetters, each a smaller one-man boat, were setting wherever they could. In the chaos it was almost impossible not to get in each other's way.

But out there on the water waiting for the horn to sound the opening, I began to see the fishing fraternity, and how groups of fishermen kept each other informed of where they were and what they were seeing. There were code words among friends that allowed Jim Tarkanen, our captain, to communicate with his close friends about where everyone was fishing and what they were seeing, all in a poker-faced tone that wouldn't give away information to anyone except their close-knit band of friends and family.

That first late afternoon, fishing was rather disappointing. We only made one set before darkness settled in. The gillnetters continued fishing into the night, but it is dangerous for a seine boat to make a set after dark. Our first set was not very successful, with only twenty-five or thirty fish brought in. Several of those were pink salmon, which Fisheries, in their wisdom, had declared off-limit, anticipating a small run that year. Pinks run earlier than the more valuable sockeye and coho salmon, and the opening was a bit later in June than usual to give the poor pink run a chance to move on before fishing started, though we still caught some. We were forced to throw those back, although after being brought on board in the net, it was highly unlikely that they would survive. There were also a couple of "smilies" in the set, large spring salmon of forty-five pounds and over. Spring have a marked, up-turned mouth in a seeming smile, but the real reason they were called "smilies" was because catching such valuable fish made us smile!

Billy Clegg made a dinner of mac and cheese while I endured teasing about my prowess with the oars on the skiff (which required standing, facing the direction I was rowing, a method previously unknown to me) and my struggles with piling corks, but I had made it through a first day of fishing. Beer and fish stories with the other seine boats anchored together for the night went on, but I was tired and retired early to my bunk in the diesel-perfumed cabin below, rocked to sleep by the wave action on the anchored boat, the sound of diesel engines humming, and increasingly inebriated conversations among our crew and those of neighbouring boats tied alongside.

Early the next morning, it was decided to leave the Straits and head up toward Gilford Island to Jim Tarkanen's favourite fishing spot, the Merry-Go-Round. I recently managed to get in touch with Jim, now eighty-three years old, who reminded me that the spot was next to Village Island, between Turnour and Gilford Islands. It was well-known to seiners as a place where salmon often schooled up, before heading for the long trip up Knight Inlet. Here, the flow of an incoming tide circled around the narrow channel between the islands, creating a merry-go-round effect that carried the schooled salmon off toward their inlet destination; hence its name among the fishermen.

Merry-Go-Round was such a popular spot that seine boats would line up to make a set in the narrow passage, each waiting their turn. Even the drum seiners used the permanent stake on the rocky shore of the little island to anchor their nets in the narrow confines of the channel.

For the drum seiners, this meant making fewer sets than they might normally be able to make. Our little table seiner, which took so long to make a set was generally unable to make more than three or four sets a day anyway, so it suited us just fine. The potential for big rewards as the fish schooled up made it good for all, and, indeed, there were hundreds if not a thousand fish in each set. But the sets once again included many pinks. It was a tremendous pain to sort through them and throw back the fish, which seemed to make up half the set.

And there was another unanticipated difficulty. After rowing Larry, the lead-line man, back to the boat, and commencing to pull corks, the boat pulled away to allow the next boat access. The power block began pulling in the net, and a kind of orange rain began pelting down on Billy Clegg who was piling the net. Though he was wearing rain gear as protection from the seawater that rained down on him as the net was spooled, Billy began exhorting, "YUCK!" and pulling orange slime off his hands.

Soon a pile of translucent orange slime piled around him, and we realized that in the net, along with a nice catch of sockeye and the pinks that needed to be thrown back, had come a bumper crop of jellyfish! Pulling like crazy on the cork line and piling it into the skiff, I also began to see jellyfish, but I mostly managed to avoid them, and my gloves protected me reasonably well against the slimy creatures. Once the net was securely piled on board and the fish sorted and brailed into the hold, we realized that the orange goo of the jellyfish was more than a nuisance. Poor Billy seemed to be sunburnt all over his face and arms. The jellyfish were armed with a biting sting that Billy must have felt everywhere the slime had touched his skin. Now, however, the other boats in line had taken their turn and it was time to go again.

Not wanting to seem squeamish or weak, Billy gamely joined in for two more sets with similar results. The fish were running at Merry-Go-Round. By that time Billy was red everywhere, but he tried to make light of it. We spent one more night on the boat, but he was clearly suffering. We had a good load of fish and hoped to make one more set in the morning, then off to Port Hardy to sell the fish at the cannery.

We made an open water set in the morning on the way to Port Hardy, but it was a disaster for me. One essential job of the skiff man was to re-connect the lead line to the cork line, which remained attached to the skiff as it was brought up over the stern at the end of the set. The lead line was detached from the skiff to purse the net. In my hurry to swab the deck of jellyfish and man the brailing net, I forgot to reattach the lead line after the set was finished. The morning set sent me and the skiff out with no lead line for the shore man to pass to the big boat. The screaming and yelling of fishermen's oaths aimed at this hapless greenhorn skiff man put me to shame.

After a long sullen sail to Port Hardy with westerly waves giving me the first sense of seasickness, with poor Billy nursing his red, swollen arms and face, we unloaded the fish, and were paid a decent amount for our three days of table seining.

I may have gone out on one or two more trips on that boat, but, clearly, I was NOT cut out for the job. And indeed, the *Broughton I* wasn't long for the world either. A year after my fishing expedition, the ship went through Seymour Narrows on a heavy rip tide, keeled over and went down, though Jim Tarkanen and his crew all survived.

I found my own niche, not in fishing, but falling back

Poster for Sointula rock band Blackfish Sound, l to r: author Kit Eakle, Dana Barton, Stephanie Eakle, John Lyon, Don McWilliam, Jamie Gunther. Artist Stuart Marshall on a childhood skill as a violinist, playing at parties, pubs and dances, often for returning fishers eager to celebrate their catch of the day with my band called Blackfish Sound.

This is the theme song I wrote for the band:

> *Let me tell you of a place*
> *We like to call 'home.'*
> *Where fishing boats wander*
> *And Orca schools roam.*
> *Water surrounds wooded isles*
> *Wet by rains year-'round*
> *This is our home—Call it*
> *Black-Blackfish Sound*

Today I am a jazz violinist living in Vancouver.

Buttercup and Coast Pilot

Ian Campbell

In 1959, my family arrived on the BC coast from an Alberta cattle ranch; it didn't take long for boats and the ocean to enter our lives. I was the youngest of three brothers. My first water adventure was at age ten, sharing the ownership with David Prosser (Gumboot Guy from the North Coast) of an eight-foot steel pontoon boat found in an irrigation pond. Later, while exploring by rowboat with my brother Tim (who much later founded Marine Link Transportation Ltd, a marine freight business), unaware of tides and currents, we learned that we had to hang on to kelp bulbs to wait for the cur-

rent to slow down and reverse to be able to return home. Our father, with no boating experience, purchased a twenty-six-foot sailboat for family sailing outings in the Gulf Islands. As an eleven-year-old I became deckhand for Dad offering day sailing charters on this very modest sailboat. We had some interesting clients such as then BC Premier W.A.C. Bennett, who left a lasting impression on me with a five-dollar tip. The other memorable client was an emerging actor called Burt Reynolds: I don't recall getting a tip, but I do remember his shapely girlfriend wearing a white bikini. Years later, my brothers and I were heading to Lasqueti, winter sailing on the classic vessel *Native Girl*, so that my brother Dane

Ian Campbell

Buttercup, a wood, gaff-rigged Tahiti Ketch built in San Pedro, California, powered by 2-cylinder Gardner.

could deliver his final payment to the boat's builder, Allen Farrell. We arrived in a snowstorm, and I was impressed by Allen running out of his cabin in bare feet through a foot of snow to greet us.

Those early experiences of boats and the lure of the BC coast led me to pursue a career with the Canadian Hydrographic Service. The purchase of my first boat, a thirty-foot wood Tahiti Ketch *Buttercup*, provided a home to live on in the days when you could hang on a mooring buoy with a stern line to the dock in front of the Empress Hotel in Victoria. It was a short walk up Government Street to go to work at the Hydrographic Office. My first summer assignment was on board the *William J Stewart* a 228-foot ship with a triple expansion steam engine and teak decks. The *Willie J*, as it was affectionately called, arrived in Victoria in 1932 from Ontario. A fine ship in its twilight years of operation, it provided luxury accommodation for surveyors, boasting a dining lounge for officers and surveyors with meals served by white-jacketed stewards. On occasion the deck crew would holystone the teak decks. The first day working in the chart room, I was shocked to look up and see we had hauled anchor and were underway with the smooth and remarkably quiet steam engine.

It's amazing to think how technology has advanced since the seventies. From the *Willie J* we were rowed ashore with survey equipment in wooden east coast dories. After setting up shore stations with tripods and flags over known control points, sounding lines would begin from the wooden launches. On board would be a coxswain, two surveyors turning horizontal sextant angles to shore stations and a third surveyor tending the paper sounder. Left and right sextant angles would be plotted with a plastic three-arm protractor giving the launch's exact location when the fix was called, and the sounder trace marked. It was an archaic but accurate method.

That summer, I got to see glimpses of the mouth of the Skeena River and experienced wild west weekends in Prince Rupert. We were then off to a survey of Masset Inlet on Haida Gwaii, all of which effectively whet my appetite for seeing more of the coast. Time off was during winter months, which meant winter sailing adventures with friends on *Buttercup* up toward Cortes Island and Desolation Sound. I recall one rip-roaring sail in a boisterous southeaster and extremely poor visibility as we crossed over the Comox bar (pre-GPS days), and realizing we were slightly off the range as we watched the sandy bottom skimming past our keel.

Work and travel on government ships expanded my desire for exploring more of the coast on my own schedule. I resigned from the government and, after making modifications to *Buttercup*, I approached the Hydrographic Service about doing contract work. A trial season doing Revisory Survey work updating and correcting charts and "Sailing Directions" between Victoria and Port Hardy was a success. After years of tiller steering in the open cockpit of a sailboat, a warm wheelhouse with coffee in hand had become a priority, then a reality with the purchase of my second boat, a wooden forty-four-foot Phil Barron power boat. This became the first of several vessels to carry the *Coast Pilot* name and be outfitted to do contract survey work. A chart cabinet to fit full-sized charts was installed in the wheelhouse. Chart corrections and additions had to be hand-inked onto plastic master copies of each chart. We set up a mobile chart dealership on board and carried a full selection of new charts with a sign in the rigging stating "Charts for

Coast Pilot, a wooden Phil Barron design, built in Sooke and powered by 471 Jimmy.

Sale." Fishermen and other mariners would stop by to purchase charts and on hearing of our survey work would report errors, omissions or corrections that they had encountered. These would be investigated or added to our work list for following seasons.

Survey work was very seasonal, and a variety of winter activities kept us busy. Both the sailboat and power boat were set up with a C licence, which allowed us to fish rock cod for the Chinese market.

One winter, an arrangement with the National Film Board permitted me to take a projector and a collection of film reels to offer movie nights at various locations. A portable generator provided power if needed. It was a fun social activity, and the reward was often a hot shower and meal invitation. One showing was at Redonda Bay to a group of prisoners in a work camp.

During a survey of Whiterock Passage, I got to know the storekeepers who ran the Surge Narrows store. They asked me if we would be interested in looking after the store while they took their winter holiday. All summer long the money any visitors that paid with American dollars would go into a big jar. Their idea of a winter holiday was to fly to Las Vegas and have fun gambling away their American funds. The store was a hub of activity on mail days with folks from Churchouse and draft-dodgers from surrounding communities coming in for mail and supplies. I think the store was one of the first to have a liquor distribution licence and popular beers and wines filled a Dutch-doored broom closet to capacity.

Gwyn Gray Hill, a well-known coastal character rumoured to be a remittance man from England, lived aboard his sailboat and would often show up alongside around five o'clock, just as supper was being prepared, to ask about a chart of some obscure part of the coast. Examining the chart and stories would usually lead to an invitation for supper. I don't recall if he ever purchased a chart. Gray Hill knew our coast better than anyone I ever met. It was a challenge to mention a bay or anchorage that he wasn't familiar with. He was a great storyteller and had a trapline of folks that he visited up and down the coast. He had a nickname for most everyone that he spoke of, rarely flattering. On his departure from supper, I often wondered what our nickname was. We had a tradition of always having a guestbook on board, a carryover from days on the ranch. A shared meal or anything more than a casual visit required a signature and comment in the guestbook. Gray Hill had very poor eyesight. His thick glasses would come off, his head lowered to within inches of the guest book, and a slow and methodical signature would appear in copperplate script.

One summer, a boater had reported hitting an "uncharted" rock on Sutil Point at the southwest corner of Cortes Island. A Friday afternoon low tide allowed a visual examination of the rock in question, confirmed by a skid mark of red bottom paint. A radio request was made to the Victoria office for additional survey control points to confirm the rock's location. On Monday we returned to record an exact position of the rock using horizontal sextant angles to shore stations, only to discover fresh blue bottom paint on the same rock. Obviously, another boater had taken a dangerous shortcut across the same reef area which was, in fact, adequately charted.

Updating "Sailing Directions" for fuel and other services was a great excuse to stop at small settlements, and one time we were requested to go into Sullivan Bay. We heard through the coastal grapevine that just a few days earlier the husband of the couple that ran the facility had been killed in a floatplane crash. We were uneasy about having to interview the widow so soon after the tragedy but were amazed by her strength and composure to carry on running their business. We never forgot and often thought of this amazing young lady. Fast forward forty-plus years: we were hitchhiking on Cortes Island to get back to our boat anchored in Cortes Bay and a lady picked us up. As we chatted on the drive across the island, she mentioned she had operated a business up in the Broughtons years ago. As we zeroed in on the location and determined it was Sullivan Bay, I asked, "Did you buy the business from the widow?" She answered: "No... I was the widow." With goosebumps rising we inadvertently drove right past Cortes Bay and our boat. We were able to tell her how in awe we were of her those many years ago.

The fourth and final boat to carry the *Coast Pilot* name was a fifty-foot Gooldrup boat built at Campbell River. Renowned for building skookum fishboats with great lines, this was one of the few pleasure boats that Mike Gooldrup built. It was for sale in Juneau, Alaska, and we were pleased to buy it and bring it back home to the Campbell River and Cortes Island area. Within hours of arriving in Campbell River, Mike and his son showed up for a visit on board. He was very proud of this one-of-a-kind boat. That vessel proved to be wonderful for living on board and continuing with our contract work.

Our enjoyment has never diminished after five decades of travelling the coast with all the amazing connections of characters and boats and favourite spots. We ended up dropping anchor in a magical spot overlooking Gorge Harbour on Cortes Island, fulfilling the dream of a property with deep water protected moorage. We now get to catch up with old cruising friends as they stop by on their way up or down the coast.

Chanson

Richard Porter

This is the story of Peter Rabbit Island. I don't remember the island's real name, but it lies somewhere up the BC coast, well north of the Salish Sea. Fog is common on that part of the coast, so you may well pass by the island without noticing its towering evergreen canopy or the little sheltered anchorage hidden around the point.

In 1974, we had moved onto the *Chanson*, our thirty-two-foot roomy and fast Brandlmayr, a locally built cedar-on-oak carvel sloop, for the summer and fall. Our crew of four consisted of myself, my then wife Barbara, our two-and-a-half-year-old daughter Aswea, and Buja, our part-wolf-but-mostly-mixed-breed canine family member who howled at whales. (He still visits in dreams.) We didn't have a clear destination, our goal being to meander slowly up the coast, living mainly off the land and sea, getting as far north as we could before the onset of winter.

We had left our home port of Maple Bay in July. I had grown up in Maple Bay and had spent my teenage summers racing and cruising the Gulf

I had to subdue the 82-pound handlined halibut with an oar before I could bring it aboard my tiny Sportyak plastic dinghy.

Islands with my friends in our small open sailboats. Now, fifteen years later and with a family, we had sailed the *Chanson* to Victoria for a refit, and were then exploring the area again, including Denman Island (where we later settled), Desolation Sound, the Broughtons and some of the mainland inlets, meandering our way northward. Cruising British Columbia's beautiful and complex coastline of islands and inlets was always full of fun and adventure. Food was easily had by dangling a fishing line or foraging the beaches for their many wild vegetables and multitude of shellfish. We often shared anchorages with other like-minded adventurers. Friendships developed over meals, drinks and stories, as we watched the sun go down.

By September, we were on our way around Cape Caution, the infamous section of exposed open Pacific that must be navigated before the sheltered waters of the Inside Passage to Alaska can be regained. Fewer seasonal sailors ventured beyond this point and a more intense wilderness experience awaited. After provisioning in Port Hardy, a day of sailing saw us pulling into a tiny, sheltered anchorage nestled between two small islands. A pre-dinner handlining from our six-foot Sportyak proved especially productive when I unexpectedly landed a huge halibut, not a small feat in such a tiny dinghy! Watching from the *Chanson* anchored close by, Barbara yelled that I was a "murderer" as I subdued it with an oar before I could bring it aboard. This was a point well-taken, as killing, even for food, has always been a difficult process for me and I had already caught more than enough fish to dry in the rigging. Nevertheless, my eighty-two-pound halibut was the catch to end all catches and, once salted down, provided us food for a month!

The *Chanson* was our beamy and fast Brandlmayr 32-foot cedar-on-oak locally built sloop we fitted out for cruising.

After a delicious halibut dinner, I rowed ashore with Buja so he could attend

On board the *Chanson*, Buja, our part-wolf-mostly-mixed-breed crew member, howls at a nearby humpback whale.

to his business. I spotted a narrow path leading through the undergrowth and into the towering evergreens. The path had obviously not been travelled for some time and was difficult to discern winding through the forest duff but, with Buja in the lead, I followed it for a distance uphill and eventually came to a small clearing in the woods. I noticed remnants of a campfire where someone must have spent the night long ago. I also spotted what looked like an old sign sticking up at an angle nearby. The paint was badly faded but, to the discerning eye the sign clearly read "Peter Rabbit Lives Here." *Aha,* I thought, *Aswea will be most interested in this!* And indeed, when we reboarded the *Chanson*, Aswea was

My two-and-a-half-year-old daughter Aswea savors the pink huckleberries Peter Rabbit left for her in a cockle shell.

very excited to hear that Buja and I had actually found Peter Rabbit's home while we were ashore.

First thing in the morning, we packed a lunch and set off up the path again. Aswea brought some fresh lettuce as a present just in case she actually met Peter Rabbit. We three excitedly followed Buja up the trail, past a weird monster tangle of roots and, a bit farther on, an even scarier opening into a deep, dark and mysterious cave. Continuing along, we finally arrived at the little clearing in the forest. Aswea's delight was palpable as she spotted the sign and I read it out to her: "'Peter Rabbit Lives Here,' it says!" So thrilling it was to happen upon the very place where Peter Rabbit actually lived! We hunted high and low to see if we could find his doorway, but to no avail. As disappointment ensued, I suggested to Aswea that she leave the lettuce by the sign. Then she and her mother could look around some trees a bit farther along while I searched on the other side of the clearing. Shortly afterwards, having had no success, we all returned to the little sign again, only to make an amazing discovery. Peter Rabbit, by nature a very shy fellow, had come and gone while we were away looking for his house! He had taken the lettuce and, in its place, left some freshly picked, delicious pink huckleberries in a beautiful cockle shell especially for Aswea! Aswea was overjoyed.

And that is why the island is called Peter Rabbit Island to this very day!

Cy Peck and Viola Gwen

John Helme

My odyssey was a personal quest for adventure and a place that aligned with my lifestyle, mirroring the experiences of many who came before me, but with a slight twist. Unlike those that escaped the craziness of the cities and suburbs, I spent my formative years on an island in the Salish Sea. Salt Spring Island is a gem in the Southern Gulf Islands that tourists and retirees have flocked to for over a century. My little island was growing rapidly in the late seventies, with new developments and a large influx of people looking for a slower pace of life. As much as I loved the beauty and comfort of Salt Spring, my friends and I felt the pull to explore new horizons and challenge ourselves in different environments.

My group of close friends was always up for an adventure! We were continually mucking around boats, beaches and the backcountry, hiking, fishing and exploring. So, it wasn't really surprising when my friend Jim bought a decommissioned ferry named the *Cy Peck*. This was the original ferry that plied the Gulf Islands including Salt Spring from 1930 to 1961.

How fun was this? Our own ferry to play with! We would use the *Cy Peck* as a giant float-ing workshop. The deck was littered with smaller boats and marine hardware, as we re-paired and restored boats. We would also clean herring roe from nets when in season on its massive decks.

The mission became clear after a couple of years: the *Cy Peck* needed to find a new home to best suit our lifestyle. Jim Russel and Finbar Mc-Millan were spearheading the project and asked if I would join them heading north with

In gumboots on the Surge dock ramp. Photo Claudia Lake

our friends Doug and Carey. I thought long and hard on this and reluctantly said no. I was twenty years old at the time and life on the island was pretty good. I was commercial fishing part time and playing in a country band. Dating life was going well. Then came a fateful day, when my father called me and said, "Cut your hair, I have a job for you on the ferries!" The decision to head north was made for me, as I had no desire to follow in my father's footsteps as an employee at BC Ferries.

That time was both exhilarating and nerve-wracking. I packed up my belongings in two days, said goodbye to my family and friends, and set off on the journey of a lifetime. As the *Cy Peck* did not have working engines, we needed a tow from another vessel. We enlisted the help of another seafaring islander, Bruce Hildred, who had recently secured a classic seventy-foot schooner, the *Anna V Fagan*, on the East Coast and brought it through the Panama Canal to Salt Spring. Bruce agreed to tow us north to a destination

The *Cy Peck*, formally known as the *Island Princess*, retired BC ferry, shown here in the early sixties.

unknown. We also had a small steel tugboat to assist.

The journey was incredible! We stopped overnight on Lasqueti and Bull Island and had a reunion of sorts with other Salt Spring islanders who had previously settled remotely and off the grid. After another day of towing, we approached Cortes Island. We believed that either Cortes, Maurelle or Read Island would be where we would find a safe remote anchorage.

As we rounded the northern tip of Cortes and entered Sutil Channel, I knew that I had found my new home. My heart and soul were captured. I was super excited to embark on this new chapter of my life filled with endless possibilities and adventures. After we dropped a 2,000-pound anchor in Quartz Bay on northern Cortes Island, I found myself falling more and more in love with the untouched beauty of that area. The crisp air, the silence, and the feeling of being completely disconnected from the modern world all captivated me. Eventually, my future partner, Beverly Hollingsworth, and I would settle in Quartz Bay. At the head of the bay, Beverly knew of an abandoned one-room cabin that we made our own and cohabitated in for our first winter together. It was basically a hunter's cabin on the beach. When I say on the beach, I mean *really* on the beach. The king tides would occasionally lap inside our door, but it was a start.

Several months later I said goodbye to almost all of my travelling Salt Spring friends as the *Cy Peck* was towed away to its next home near Ladysmith, leaving Beverly and me in solitude five miles from the closest road.

I will never forget the stillness and silence I encountered that year we were alone in Quartz Bay, punctuated only by the howling of the wolves from Von Donop Inlet [Háthayim] to Carrington Bay. They regularly visited our yard and bay feeding at the seaside. At the time our only transport was an eighteen-foot freight canoe. We would paddle the five miles to Coulter Bay, where we kept a car to get supplies from Whaletown or Campbell River. Needless to say, the weather often prevented us from getting to or from the bay.

I couldn't help but wonder if it was realistic to pursue a life here in the future. Would I be able to make a living in such a remote and rugged environment? Would I be able to adapt to the challenges of living off the grid and relying on my own resourcefulness to survive?

The following spring was eventful. We secured an off-grid cabin in Coulter Bay (four kilometres from the road). Beverly was pregnant with Auraly at the time, and we wanted to be closer to town. Being off the grid did not mean we were without amenities. We had the best propane lights, an airtight stove for heat, a cookstove and an outside wood-fired bathtub. We even had a mini six-inch TV run off a car battery. With the antennae, we only got the CBC channel, so we reserved it for Saturday cartoons and Hockey Night in Canada. When Auraly was two years old and after our daughter Kiya Rose was born, we moved to Whaletown. Our son Hamish was born in a cabin in Whaletown Bay.

The lifestyle is not for everyone as it can be a tremendous amount of work to survive and sustain. I was in my early twenties and quite strong. From an anchorage, packing babies into a skiff to the beach can be challenging as well as transporting a myriad of things, such as fuel, food, supplies, diapers, and not to forget firewood! Also, loading the vessel when picking up in town everything we needed for at least a few weeks at a time.

That spring of 1979, I received some other good news. I would soon become a proud owner-operator of a thirty-four-foot wooden gillnet/troller for fishing salmon. After a couple of seasons on the Skeena River fishing sockeye, I wrangled a lease-to-buy deal from Canfisco. I purchased the sturdy *Viola Gwen*, a Wahl boat built for the Port Edward gillnet fleet. I immediately installed gurdies, poles and davits to troll for salmon as well. I would now be able to netfish sockeye in the Skeena River in the summer and troll for chinook salmon near home in the spring. Not only that: we now had safe transport when children were on board.

Having been used to an active social life on Salt Spring Island, I was concerned there would be a vacuum by moving to such a remote place. This was not the case! At first, I filled the void with the odd friend from home who would visit for extended periods of time, as they loved the lifestyle. Missing camaraderie and music, Beverly and I would host parties on our beach for our local friends. What was unique about these parties in remote places was the fact that folks did not show up just for a few hours in the evening—they would stay for at least a day or two and sometimes more. I loved this lifestyle as it gave us plenty of time together to play music, feast, get high and share life stories. Feast we did! Our parties almost always featured fresh salmon, crab, prawns, cod, clams and venison on an open fire on the beach. We even once shared a porpoise, which had tragically died in the Johnstone Strait, caught in my gillnet. (I had tried desperately to save it, but it drowned before we could disentangle it. I was heartbroken but didn't want to waste its death.) We would play music to the wee hours of the night on acoustic instruments and drums that we would fashion from almost anything at hand.

This led to me organizing live music at our local venue whenever possible. I would import my good friends Tom and Sue and their kick-ass band Club Mongo from my hometown to play at the Gorge Hall. This was a win-

"Day-after" party at Surge Narrows. Photo Claudia Lake

win-win. My southern friends and their band would come to Cortes to play and visit, my northern friends would enjoy live dance music and I would be able to play with the band for a song or two. We took it a step further by organizing and playing in Surge Narrows. Our inaugural trip was iconic as we were the first band or electric group to play in the hall. Everyone from miles around showed up in support when we played there. It was a true community effort, packing the PA and instruments from the boat, from the dock, up a hill, to the hall. We would fire up the old generator and the band would play until the early morning hours.

I remember one day after a gig in Surge when we all needed to return to Cortes, but unfortunately the fog had set in. It was truly pea soup that day. Seeing that the only working radar was on the *Viola Gwen,* we rafted and towed up to a half dozen vessels across Sutil Passage at two knots to Whaletown to get them home safely. This was the kind of meaningful bonding experiences for all of us who lived remotely, giving us a sense of community and friendship that we still share today.

Although much of our seafaring adventures sound romantic and fun, I have personally survived two shipwrecks at sea and have lost some very close friends while fishing over fifteen years. The ocean is a tough mistress, but I consider myself extremely lucky. Despite the many uncertainties I encountered, one thing is certain: my journey had fueled a passion for adventure, exploration and living a simpler, more intentional life. That was something worth pursuing, no matter where the journey ultimately led. My odyssey may have been a personal quest, but it had become a journey of self-discovery and growth, shaping me into the person I have become as well as the father I was meant to be. Two of my children continued my legacy by going to sea. My son, Hamish, went on to become a mega-yacht captain. He is based in Fort Lauderdale, Florida, and just finished a Mediterranean and Adriatic Sea adventure. My daughter Kiya Rose visited dozens of countries on a private yacht, globetrotting for several years as an onboard steward. I am delighted they may have inherited some of my adventurous spirit.

Daisy Mae II

Colin Ritchie

My interest in boats came about because my father was in the British navy, and boats of one sort or another were always part of my life. The first I remember was when Dad was posted as naval attaché in the British embassy in Tokyo and we had a sampan with a small Seagull outboard motor, which we used on an inland lake. Then, shortly before I immigrated to Canada at seventeen, after finishing school, our family had the use of a thirty-foot sailboat on the River Shannon in Ireland.

The Canadians were stationed where we lived during the war, and they ended up marrying a lot of the English girls. One was a school chum of my mother's. They had a big ranch just west of Calgary, where I ended up for a year. I

Taking a breather while handlogging in Nepah Lagoon, in the Broughtons.

then immigrated legally. I attended the University of Calgary, which was one big party, from which I graduated in 1970. After moving to the BC coast, I then joined a bunch of pals on a back-to-the-land trip at a place we called Mudslide, northeast of Prince George, with dreadful weather. Eventually the coast drew me back and I ended up on Denman Island.

I acquired a couple of boats while there: a thirty-foot tug called the *Island Scout* and then a sixty-footer named the *Island Planet*. After a while, I went to work in a small logging camp in Muchalat Inlet on the west coast of Vancouver Island, out of Gold River, to make enough money to put hydro in on my Denman property. While there, I bought a thirty-six-foot East Coast style lobster boat, the *Daisy Mae II*, which had been built by an old logger

Daisy Mae II pulling in to Echo Bay after towing logs to Scott Cove Logging Camp, in the Broughtons.

on Reid Island. In my glorious naivety, I thought I might try beachcombing/log salvaging but quickly learned that was out of the question. The West Coast is wild.

A Denman Island friend, John Kirk, who was handlogging at Glendale Cove in Knight Inlet, spurred my interest in this form of logging. In 1966, the provincial government had legalized the use of boats to yard logs off shoreline claims. With *Daisy Mae* and a couple of pals, I started exploring the so-called jungles of the Broughton Archipelago, and the foreshores, coastal inlets, and islands around Kingcome and Drury Inlets, looking for handlogging claims. A few days into the trip we noticed a small opening along the shoreline in Mackenzie Sound. The opening was called Roaring Hole Rapids (we called it Terror Trench!) and, having a chart datum depth of only three-and-a-half feet, it was spooky. *Daisy Mae* had a shallow draught, and I usually went in at high slack. It led into the most beautiful lagoon called Nepah which was to be my home off and on for the next seventeen years. One winter I was frozen in for nine days but had a good supply of books.

Each timber claim comprised a mile of shoreline. I had six claims in the lagoon over the years. I worked alone most of the time, using the simplest hand-operated equipment, consisting of chokers, a hand jack, chainsaws, log chains and tow lines, and the *Daisy Mae* for yarding the logs. Gravity and ingenuity lent valuable assistance. I had to make sure to batten everything down inside the boat before yarding logs off the hillside. If the log got hung up the boat would come to a grinding halt, and everything inside would go flying.

Grizzly bears and cougars were everywhere. In the early years, a girl-friend I had met in New Zealand came with her two children to help out. We roughed it, living on rice and fish. She ran the boat standing on a toolbox to reach the controls. One night while the kids were sleeping in a shack I had built on land, they were awakened by scratching and growls. The next day there were claw marks ten feet up the tree next to the shack. We quickly moved the shack onto a small log float.

Towing through narrow channels in the middle of a dark, cold winter night to run with the tides was no fun, as I had no radar or depth sounder, just a spotlight to light up the shore. My only radio contact with the outside world was with the Alert Bay Coast Guard Radio and Henry Speck at the native village of Hopetown, which was quite close by. The folks at Nimmo Bay in the neighbouring inlet were just getting their operation going, so we would get together every once in a while.

Yarding logs off the hillside in Nepah Lagoon.

I would make up a boom and would then tow it to the sawmill at Telegraph Cove on Vancouver Island if the weather was with me, or tow six miles to Sullivan Bay, where tugs with larger booms heading to Vancouver would pick it up. Good friends at Sullivan Bay, Pat and Lynn, provided home-cooked meals and showers. In the summer I would sometimes tow to Echo Bay and in the winter months to Caviar Cove in Drury Inlet.

A few years later, I brought the *Virginia Hope*, a seventy-two-foot ex-rumrunner, to Nepah Lagoon to live on and tow with. My largest tow of full-length cedar logs consisted of eight strings, with fifteen cedar logs apiece, strung 400 metres behind me, which I delivered to Scott Cove next to Echo Bay. The trip was memorable because of many friends tied alongside as we began the journey. I had two prawn boats, two sailboats and friends' kayaks all over the deck and, as the fog lifted, they cast off and continued on their way, slowly dispersing as I kept chugging along.

I would go on holidays for a month or two, and when I was broke, I'd get an advance from the log broker in Vancouver who bought from the small gyppo loggers. I would then stock up with provisions, cans of Habitant pea soup, Irish stew, barbecued baked beans, and Bisquick mix, as I had no refrigeration. I would store my fresh vegetables and fruit in the hold. My last stop for supplies was in Alert Bay for fuel before heading into the bush again for a couple of months.

In the later years I bought a floathouse from a friend who had lost his wife and child in a floatplane crash. This made it easier for friends to visit. Bobby Lamont, who had been a high-line log salvager and then switched to handlogging, had the *Gale Winds* and would come with his wife to help me out. She was a fantastic cook, and they were both great company.

I had my fair share of close calls yarding wood over the years. One day, as we started pulling on a big log, it got sheared sideways around a large standing tree and its weight started pulling the boat back to the shoreline at an alarming rate. When this happens, the natural inclination is to give the boat more power, but this merely creates a hole under the stern. Thus, more water starts piling on the stern deck as the boat is getting dragged backwards. The throttle has to be jockeyed very carefully to prevent the boat from sinking. Usually, the tow line burns into the back of the standing tree and the jammed log eventually comes to a halt. That's when the work really starts.

Handlogging was considered a tough and often dangerous operation, but I learned as I went along. It was very satisfying and a huge adventure. I was very lucky. I was pretty much the last gyppo logger in the area. The new forest practice code had come into effect, and I didn't fit into the parameters anymore, so I called it a day.

I had gotten to know Alert Bay on my fuel stops. I had always liked restoring old wooden buildings and I found a plethora of them there. I restored an old warehouse on pilings over the beach and turned it into a hotel, naming it the Seine Boat Inn in honour of the boats that made this community. I also bought a couple of old seiners with the intent of preserving some of the last of the fishing fleet in the North Island. I continue to work on restoration projects to this day in Alert Bay. I've had a wonderful and lucky life and made a lot of fantastic friends on this coast.

Gallant Girl

Michael Hawkes

Our north Pacific neighbours, the Japanese, use the honorific "Maru" in the names of their seagoing vessels. I always assumed it pointed to the love and care poured into them, to their sacred task of keeping mariners safe when out in them, and to the respect that merits.

In full swing at the Nimpkish Hotel. Photo Rick James

Here, we do something similar when giving our beloved vessels feminine attributes. The *Gallant Girl*, a gem of a boat, deserves an honorific: the name *Gallant* says it all. Although born a landlubber I always felt secure in the boat's embrace.

I came to Canada, aged twenty-one, in 1960. Heeding the romantic advice of the day to "go west young man," as soon as I could I hitchhiked to Vancouver. In the early seventies I found myself with family in Alert Bay where my wife, Miki, taught school. In 1974 we bought an old house in Sointula and settled into the pastoral bliss of Malcolm Island in those glory days. For about five years I worked as a tree planter and deck-handed on several of the local seine boats.

While seining in the Johnstone Strait, I had seen on many occasions a salty-looking boat cutting effortlessly through the fleet and had admired its lines and rugged seafaring appearance. A classic workboat, built in 1963 in Nova Scotia specifically to pack herring. A heavy built wooden vessel with an 8/74 Jimmy (General Motors) diesel for power, a very fine wave-splitting bow, a finely crafted canoe stern and wheelhouse aft were its distinguishing features. In the very early seventies Ed Gallant had brought it through the Panama Canal and up to BC with the intention of fishing tuna off the West Coast.

Gallant Girl—an early incarnation.

In 1979, salmon fishing in Johnstone Strait was at its peak, and returns to the Fraser had been good for a couple of years. In that year, I saw the *Gallant Girl* was up for sale and I conceived the idea of being a collector or packer in the straits. With the help of loans and a mortgage I was able to buy it. Between the years of 1979 and 1996 I had the great pleasure, pride and responsibility of owning, operating and maintaining this sixty-five-foot beauty. During those years, the *Gallant Girl* became a ubiquitous presence on the herring and salmon fishing grounds. For as long as there were openings in any part of the coast the *Gallant Girl* was there, from the early sockeye runs in Alberni Inlet or in the Prince Rupert area to the snaggly chum of Esperanza Inlet in November.

The boat was fitted with radar, a depth sounder, a compass and a very well-stocked chart table. The many willing young deckhands, many of them greenhorns looking for adventure, who crossed its decks during those years learned dead reckoning, to read and interpret the amazingly detailed charts and, most importantly, to collate the information on the charts to what was there in front of their eyes, or at least outlined by the radar. They were required to do three-hour wheel watches and, considering the vast amount of travelling required, it is to their credit that we never had any accidents and never went seriously astray.

In April 1986, we were cash buying for North Sea Products (NSP). They had a couple of high-line fishermen who wanted to take advantage of a ten-day halibut opening in Haida Gwaii. With Ken Reid, my right hand, number one deckhand during herring seasons for several years, and Tony Berger, a gill-netter from Mitchell Bay, we set off to cross Hecate Straits. Pine Island at 279 degrees, to Cape St. James abeam ten hours later. Stopping en route for a dip in the hot springs, we made our way to Queen Charlotte City [Daajing Giids].

The next day we negotiated the notorious Skidegate Narrows and made way to Tartu Inlet where we met the *Diane Louise* and took aboard 12,000 pounds of fish. We never did hear from the other NSP boat that we were supposed to meet. Anchored up at Langara Island [Kiis G̲waay], the most northerly and westerly point of the Islands, we heard on channel 16, the coastguard channel, that a 7.7 earthquake on Adak Island in the Aleutians threatened to send a tsunami our way. With the understanding that it is safer to be off the continental shelf, we hauled anchor and headed west out into the wide Pacific, donning our cumbersome survival suits, and battening down the hatches and everything else on deck as we went. The ocean was a leaden grey and glassy flat, a rare and unexpected condition at any time of year. It looked ominous and didn't bode well.

We were to be the first Canadians to meet the dreaded waves. After a couple of hours' travel we stopped and sat with bated breath, eyes peeled to the west and waited, not knowing what to expect. About three hours passed at high alert before the radio announced a cancellation of the synopsis and we could safely return to our anchorage at Langara.

In a celebratory mood, we took the next day off and hiked across the peninsula to the spectacular and pristine beaches on the west side of the northern tip of Graham Island. Worrying somewhat about the lack of fish aboard, we made our way south again to Rennel Sound, and back though the Narrows to Skidegate. The all-too-brief season was nearly over, our 12,000 pounds at twenty-five cents a pound might cover the cost of fuel and grub, and we were at least fifty-two hours of travel time from home. Woe was us!

The *Simon Fraser*, whose skipper, Dale, had been my main rival in the fiercely competitive cash buying business, was also tied to the dock, virtually empty. The ten-day opening had been a bust. Not wanting to share in the gloom, Tony had taken off to explore the nighttime offerings of Queen Charlotte City, leaving us to it, me wondering how I was going to pay them and Ken wondering if he would get paid. Although already springtime farther south, it began to snow, large soft flakes that quickly melted on deck. A bleak night lay ahead with a long trip across open seas to follow. We tried to get some sleep, but had the radio on low, tuned to 78a, the fishermen's channel. At about three a.m. we heard an indistinct mayday call. The *Lorinda B*, a seiner with 48,000 pounds of halibut aboard, had hit a rock in Skidegate Narrows and was calling for a packer to offload onto before it sank. "Here we are, buddy. The *Gallant Girl* with ample room for all your fish. Standing by."

Halibut are big fish. Working through the snow blizzard, Ken and I with their crew quickly transferred the load and, by the time Tony returned for breakfast, we were riding low in the water and the damaged seiner was

In the straits: Ernie Kiss on drum, me as beachman, Rick James skiffman, 1977. Photo courtesy Rick James

safely on a nearby grid. I have to admit to gloating at seeing my rival pacing the dock as we worked.

We had been commissioned to take the fish to Bellingham, in the United States. After a long, fraught, rather haphazard crossing of Hecate Sound, we pulled into the safety of Beaver Cove, offloaded 12,000 pounds and headed south down Johnstone Strait. I am sure that transporting and selling Canadian fish in the US would ordinarily require formalities of some sort but, being oblivious of the rules, we trucked blithely on through and, by six o'clock on the third day after taking the fish, we off-loaded and, with great relief, were paid and free to go home.

Looking back with the perspective that comes with retirement, I am struck by the unselfconsciously heroic nature of many of those long-gone endeavours. For the thousands of men and women who commit themselves to the unpredictable wildness of our magnificent coast, week by week, through tempestuous circumstances, natural and otherwise, I have the deepest respect and admiration. Every week, indeed, every day, seafaring working men and women face challenges that their landlubbing compatriots could only imagine in their wildest dreams. I believe that such intensive struggle in the bosom of the natural world builds incredible bonds of community spirit in which both camaraderie and co-operation flourish despite the competitive nature of the work.

In my own case I am positive that the spirit [Maru] of the vessel I was married to has enriched me and my life in more ways and to a greater extent than I could possibly put to words.

Haida

Robert DeVault

My introduction to Nootka Sound was as inauspicious as it was dramatic. Alfie Styan's forty-two-foot troller, the *Sea Maid*, went down twenty-two kilometres off Estevan Point at midnight, leaving us in a seven-foot dinghy in rolling seas in late November 1972. We rowed all night, all morning, and by one o'clock we were within sight of Nootka Light. The lightkeeper saw us and launched his speedboat to rescue us.

Two years later, a collection of friends and relatives formed a company and bought an island at Nuchatlitz, and I soon made the journey to Nootka again, in my own boat, the *Haida*. Thus began a chapter that has occupied most of my life.

Even though I was born and raised in the city, I was always happier in the wilds. My family liked hiking and camping, so I was entirely comfortable and confident on my own or with others. I joined the hiking club in university, and always felt reluctant to return from an outing. A part of me seemed to be looking for a way out. I don't feel courageous for taking the road less travelled; more like I'm just okay with avoiding things I don't like. The Vietnam war was a good reason to leave the US and get into the University of British Columbia (UBC), but I also liked Canada and its possibilities.

I didn't seem to fit in at UBC, and my wife and I could barely afford the $110 rent in Vancouver, so we looked around and ended up buying a shack on Annacis Channel from a fisherman for $500. The nice little community on Dyke Road in Queensborough is all gone now. Soon it became apparent I was not going to thrive at UBC,

Bob on the roof. Photo Monique Faivre

The *Haida* at Nuchatlitz, late seventies, had a one-cylinder Easthope and I ran it for fourteen years, everywhere from Vancouver to Brooks Peninsula.

and I was ready for a change. Two things had become clear to me: that my education was preparing me for life in some corporation somewhere, and that I was always happiest in a natural setting. Not seeing a clear resolution to this conflict and having spent the last seventeen years in school, I was ready to try something really different. I had no idea that a place like Bamfield existed until I went on a field trip there while I was still at UBC. Everything about it was intriguing: an actual fishing village like in a storybook, the Pacific Ocean, boats of all kinds, even dugout canoes, and resourceful folks living their own lives, governed by the weather and tides.

Our relationship was ending anyway, so in December of 1969 I left everything I couldn't get into my backpack, headed to Port Alberni and took the *Lady Rose* passenger ferry to Bamfield. I soon located a rental house for thirty dollars a month and settled in. Over the next few months, I found a few small jobs, and by fishing season I was deck-handing on trollers. It was amazing! I had enough money, interesting work, and lots of free time to explore. I realize now that I also had the rare opportunity to learn from all the old-timers about life on the coast. It was truly an apprenticeship for what was to come.

I bought the *Haida* in 1970, while it was resting on the beach in Bamfield: cost me one hundred dollars and some work. Built at Bidwell Boat works in Vancouver in 1934 and named *Brenda D*, reportedly for

Bidwell Boat Works, the builder's small brass sign on the *Haida*. Photo Robert DeVault

the Skeena gillnet fishery, it had been chartered for trolling until time and neglect caught up to it. At twenty-eight feet long, but only twenty-eight inches deep, it glided along easily with the 7-9 Easthope chuffing at 600 RPM. Local old-timers took pity on me and showed me how to make repairs. Mr. Wickham gave me a few pieces of one-by-two-inch oak for ribs, and Pat Kelly let me use some old pipes for a make-shift steamer. Roald Ostrom at the machine shop loaned me a honer to clean up the cylinder and I put in new rings and valves. In those days, everybody seemed to know the routine of engine maintenance; my education had not prepared me to cut shims from an old phone book to adjust the main bearing clearance on the Easthope. With the new rings, I was not strong enough to turn the flywheel to start the motor, but a very strong young fisherman named Amos got it going for me, and it didn't take long to break it in. Hand-starting one of those things must be a lost art by now.

For the next fourteen years, that old boat was central to my life. I didn't own a car. It took six hours to get to Port Alberni by water, but I could live on the boat when in town. Time spent at 5.5 knots, cruising through a wooded fjord to the gentle throb of an engine that pushes the boat along two feet with every power stroke is a different kind of time from time spent clutching a steering wheel, dodging potholes on the Bamfield road.

Over the next few years, with the development of the Bamfield Marine Station in 1972, the town started to change. New people were moving in, and property became worth something. I was repeatedly evicted and ended up buying a floathouse that was also evicted. It became clear to many of us young folks that we would need to buy land if we wanted to settle. Some of us attempted to stake Crown land, of which there was a lot. Even though there was still a Homestead Act, it became clear that the government was not awarding any of these applications, though we were never told why.

We couldn't do much from Bamfield, so we moved to Port Alberni for a year to earn a bit of money and do research. We looked all over the coast and made a dozen offers, but the only one that was accepted was the bid for private land on an island in Nuchatlitz—a fifty-six-acre island romantically named Lot 435. It's a terrific location, but the island is covered with old-growth timber and there is no soil at all. We needed to pool our very limited resources to come up with the $35,000 down payment. Legal advice was to form a company, then issue shares for our house sites, awkward at times, but it has worked for fifty years.

So, in 1974, a group of friends and relatives hoping to own our own piece of paradise formed Nuchatlitz Enterprises Inc. Most of us were young folks who just wanted to try a different life from living in the city. We had been earning our money in the traditional coastal ways: fishing, forestry, clam digging. It wasn't that hard to find work if you were willing to take what was offered. We felt confident enough to commit to joining forces and taking the leap into land ownership. We had to divide the land twelve ways, which meant we each had to come up with almost $7,000 somehow over the next few years. We succeeded in that, though some of the original shareholders found the life too challenging and sold out. But nearly fifty years later, half of the original owners still have their shares!

I think there was an element of nostalgia in the back-to-the-land movement of the seventies. People today might not understand the fear of nuclear war and the apparent unwillingness of "the Establishment" to forsake the arms race in favour of peace, social justice and sustainability. Even with some progress in civil rights and a budding environmental movement, the choices offered to us seemed embedded in an endless cycle of growth and resource consumption, and an increasing detachment, not just from nature, but from the very realities of existence. Our loose circle of friends lacked any unifying ideology, and we tended to be almost perversely independent, but we shared an admiration of the people who settled the coast before us. They seemed to be living within their means, however humbly, and if they had to work hard to keep their boats going and gardens growing, there was a level of engagement with their world that seemed more in line with what we believed to be a rich and benign lifestyle.

We somehow managed to agree to, or at least accept, a division of our land into twelve parcels according to, more or less, our wishes. I required a southern exposure, even though it meant my access was a bit limited by the tide. I had had a northern exposure in Bamfield and hated to be in the shade on a cold, clear day.

A degree in engineering might seem like a dubious qualification, but I do seem to be a pretty good solver of practical problems, even those I create myself. Before leaving Port Alberni, I read some books about house construction. I bought lumber and reject plywood, insulation, plastic, tarpaper, nails, an airtight heater, basic tools, and a small generator. That and most of our gear and possessions were loaded into a Budget truck and driven to the Uchuck shed at Gold River. After returning the truck, we packed what was left, including the cat, into our VW beetle, and headed over the Tahsis road in the snow. I can scarcely believe the way we had to do things then. We had to anchor the *Haida* in the bay, launch the tiny Sportyak dinghy and ferry all our stuff to the beach. I can't remember how I got the table saw ashore. At least we had our youthful strength and innocence, tons of time, and the energy that comes from living a dream.

My girlfriend and I moved out in December of 1974 and lived in a tent cobbled together with sheets of plastic, trees and poles. Sometimes snow would fall off the trees and knock the condensation off our clear ceiling, giving us a spritz we could have done without. But we had an airtight "hippy-burner" stove, a cat and, unlike the homeless of today, we owned the ground under our feet.

I don't think that I was alone in my state of mind. On the one hand, the world seemed headed for Hell and only looking for faster ways of getting there. On the other, though we had nothing, not even prospects, we had land, energy, freedom and resources, only limited by our ability to use them. This was my happy place. To wake up to a new day, without obligations to anybody, surrounded by beauty and real-world challenges to work on, like lighting a fire and hopping back into a warm bed to plan my next move. Each day would develop according to our most immediate needs, considering the weather and the tide, and lesser concerns like food or money.

After a few weeks spent settling into our tent and clearing a small site for the cabin, the *Uchuck III* delivered our freight. The nice folks on the reserve let us use their float for the drop, and it took many trips to get it all ashore. The cabin was only 330 square feet, and we were in it only nine days later. True, it was sitting on stumps, and only had a plastic roof, but it was fully insulated and had a nice dry, level, plywood floor. The ensuing months were focussed on finding shake blocks and other materials to finish the job.

The following fall, we went to work in Tahsis, where there were two big sawmills that always seemed to be looking for workers. It wasn't the nicest situation, but with the provided meals and bunkhouses, we were able to save a lot of money while living there through the winter months. We repeated this pattern over many years. The personnel guy at the mill would let me know they didn't like workers who didn't stay, and I would resist the temptation to point out that the previous personnel guy had said the same thing.

For many years, the *Haida* was the best we had for the 32-km trip from Nuchatlitz to Tahsis, so I took along anybody who needed a trip to town. There were about eight people living out here, but it was very fluid. The 7-9 Easthope went through a third of a gallon of gas every hour, though it took three hours to make the trip. A gallon was 34 cents. Photo T.T. Sr.

In between mill stints, I did a bit of cod fishing on my C licence, but it never added up to much. In Kyuquot, they offered three-and-a-half cents a pound for yelloweye rockfish, five cents if dressed, but I could get a dollar a pound for ling cod at the dock.

Over the next decade, mostly a bachelor again, I worked little by little to improve and expand my little empire. I drew up many plans and executed some. I built a sawmill, a big workshop and a replacement for the aged *Haida*. Then came the oyster farm and, finally, a nice big house. I have had a lot of time to think. Sitting pretty now, but somehow, I'm seventy-eight years old, and starting to feel it!

It's impossible to say who might have influenced my choices. Of course, my parents were key, with their love and support and confidence in me. My time in Bamfield, though short, had put me in touch with a different sort of folks: not very educated in the usual sense, they knew what they needed to. They lived life on their own terms—some worked hard and prospered, others were content to get by. For nearly one hundred years, the town developed in isolation, and the people were used to solving their own problems. They knew boatbuilding, engine work, machine work, welding, fishing, home repairs, how to grow gardens and fruit trees, and how to put up firewood. They ran the town power plant, marine ways, gas station. The local hardware, machine shop and boat ways had an amazing breadth and depth of knowledge and were always there to help. There was a man named Johnny Vanden, who lived alone and voluntarily stopped fishing every season when he had enough (John thought "enough" was $2,500!). He then tended his garden and trees, boat and house. I would meet him on the trail to Brady's Beach and listen to his quiet sense of wonder and gratitude.

It's all different now. I could not do today what I did then. You can't even buy fuel in most places anymore. There is very little available work, and no land to purchase. I will never know what my life might have been if I had chosen a different path, but I certainly have no regrets for the wonderful years I have spent on the coast.

Inlet Vagabond

Jamie Taylor

I guess it all started back in the early seventies. Victoria Douglass Pear changed her last name and we officially embarked on a continuation of our high school romance. Chasing adventure, we bought a fifty-year-old Monterey troller, one of those picturesque clippers that grace so many San Francisco postcards. Some say to rename a boat is bad luck, but I have never relied on good or bad luck. Previous owners (hippies) had named her *Fukarwe* after their desperate radio call in fog, "Where the fuck are we?!" It felt appropriate

as I painted *Victoria* on its cute little transom. We stripped it from bow to stern, replaced the old one-lunger Hicks with a forty hp Buda diesel, and re-rigged. When I cleared the harbour in Princeton, California, I was as green—literally and figuratively—as the wide-open sea. "Lady Victoria!" old Italian fishermen would call to me on the radio, as the fleet headed for the grounds. I was eager to learn what it takes to catch the flashing salmon. I had no radar or GPS. I used an old aircraft Loran, a depth sounder, charts, compass, my wristwatch, and apprehension to lay course. I never made

Vicki and me in front of the *Victoria*: livin' on love and boats.

much money in those early years but, after crossing the Potato Patch under the Golden Gate Bridge and running for cover over the Noyo River bar with my boat and my hair standing on end, I learned some of what all greenhorns must.

Having come of age in a time of great social upheaval, Vicki, me and my two older brothers with their wives and kids, all threw in together, determined to find a meaningful life. Oregon, Washington, the wilderness, a "place in the boonies" became our clarion call. We soon became disheartened to realize we couldn't afford a suitable destination near the ocean and on a lark, we dabbled with the idea of going to Canada. The very word stirred my blood and kept me awake at night. After a few inquiries we received an encouraging reply from an agent in Campbell River, BC. My brothers and I were soon soaring in a float plane over the woods and swirling inlets of an enchanting foreign land. The area near the mouth of Knight Inlet from Wells Passage to the Broken Islands looks like a flooded mountain range, with just the forested tops breaching for air. The larger islands and wider inlets to the north and south are very different from this tangled maze that the towboaters call "The Jungles." After landing at a few places near Minstrel Island, we happened on the lovely natural harbour at Berry Island. We were soon all standing in our new Black Diamond gumboots (locally called Kingcome slippers) on a magical beach, in front of our new (old) homestead house overlooking Farewell Harbour. So named when in 1870, Royal Navy Commander Daniel Pender weighed anchor aboard the famous HMS *Beaver* before heading back to England. He had "fared well" and was "bidding farewell" to the BC coast.

My two brothers, with wives and girlfriends, Vicki and I, three kids, one toddler, and three dogs all lived in one house, the only inhabitants of Berry Island. Sound like fun? We were a motley crew, rich with optimism but savvy poor. The ripe, potent smell of a low tide beach, the brooding, mysterious treeline, the calls of ravens and eagles, all informed us that we had found our place in the wilderness. The year was 1978.

After shooting the wad on the property, tools, the move, old rebuilt outboard motors and supplies, we arrived broke, with one old pickup truck loaded like it rolled off a *Grapes of Wrath* movie set. Old Fred Wastell from the antiquated mill in Telegraph Cove, took us and all our stuff out to Berry Island on his good ship *Gikumi*. Always a help to all coasters, he once gave me eight hundred dollars of fuel on a handshake. For the next four years we would park the truck in Telegraph Cove, disconnect the battery, and commute across Johnstone Strait, through the Blow Hole, across

Blackfish Sound, through West Pass and into Farewell Harbour. The old place looked pretty good after some of those crossings and the woodstove felt even better.

Bente, one brother's wife, and Vicki had spent many weeks planning food supplies and such, in preparation for our adventure. They brought several twenty-litre plastic pails full of food: beans, corn, rice, flour, sugar and other staples, as well as cases of canned goods. These all held us in good stead. I had supplied all the tools and gear gleaned from garage sales, pawn shops, and second-hand stores.

With no running water in the dry season, we packed jerry cans of water from town. Vicki used to soak diapers in salt water before washing in fresh. Easier said than done considering her washing machine was an old wringer run by a pull-start gas motor, less than pleasant, especially in winter. While brothers and their girlfriends and wives alternately came and went, Vicki was steadfast and continuously working. All meals for ten people were prepared on an oil cookstove. This is just a snippet of the challenges and turmoil that Vicki persevered through.

After a couple of neighbourly trades, we wound up with a fine fourteen-foot Gregor aluminum skiff, with a ten hp outboard. It pays to be smart in a small boat and I had a lot to learn about this rocky, tide-swept coast where sixteen feet of saltchuck can disappear in six hours, then so surely to return. I told our gang to remember that when you venture below the high-water mark, you have your head in the lion's jaws. If a rolled log or boulder pins you, there would be no reasoning with the incoming tide. Try to plan to have the tide and current in your favour. I learned early to avoid tide rips or conditions of wind bucking tide, when the wind generates waves that oppose the tidal current. I'll never forget once crossing Johnstone Strait into Weynton Passage in a gale. Slipping along in the trough of the waves, slowing and turning into the big ones, all was well until it wasn't. My boat half-filled with water taught me a valuable lesson in avoiding those conditions if I could.

I beachcombed all my firewood in those years. Pulling logs off the beach and towing them home was one of my favourite pastimes. The first big fir log I got was a primal experience: four feet across, twenty feet long, gun-barrel straight. In hindsight it really should have been sawn for lumber. It was perched on the shelving, rocky shore of Swanson Island. I sweated and swore for three days to float it off. It finally floated free, but only barely. As I very slowly pulled for West Pass and home, I marvelled at how little of it showed above water. My reverie was suddenly interrupted when,

Moving too much junk, crib, baby, nephews and dreams on a log raft.

from the hidden realm below, a tall black fin towered above me. A massive bull orca, longer than my skiff, slowed alongside not six feet from me. Fear struck like a blow to my chest. I froze in awe as he steadily submerged, clearly visible far below the glassy surface. It was the greatest expression of power I had or have ever seen.

After beaching the log in front of the house, I began bucking and splitting with glee. What a find! Free for the effort! The sea provides! Firewood solved! Vicki pushed the first wheelbarrow up to the house and into the woodstove it went. While I was splitting the next round, she leaned out of the kitchen window and said with a puzzled look, "It's making a funny noise." We soon learned what was not so funny after all. Absolutely water-logged (which was why it had floated so low), it was hissing loudly as water bubbled from the ends of each piece. To say that it burned poorly would be an understatement, and the adage "where there's smoke there's fire" didn't apply either. Though nothing that a year in a dry woodshed wouldn't fix, it was just one of the many hard-won lessons of Berry Island. Vicki always said she became a good fire maker by learning on wet wood.

Many people helped us during those early years. The Cooks put us up in Alert Bay when we were storm-bound. Our neighbour on nearby Swanson Island, a renowned Doukhobor, had invented the Alaskan chainsaw mill and taught me how to mill logs into lumber. We sometimes stayed with other friends in Beaver Cove, who regaled us with coastal stories and taught me how to run tide and wind. The legendary Billy Proctor made the rounds in his sturdy *Twilight Rock*, offering fish, help and rides. His well-known gifts of keen observation and capacious memory belied his backwoods manner.

We cast about for business ideas to sustain us. We settled on a self-ill-advised plan to purchase a power barge. We were to freight supplies and equipment to outport homesteads, resorts and camps from roughly Wells Passage north to Campbell River. When the *Inlet Vagabond* arrived to load a D4 Caterpillar bulldozer we had sold to Billy Proctor, it was for sale. It was eighty-five feet of massive wooden timbers. The sides and collision bulkheads were through bolted twelve-by-twelves. The bottom and deck were planked athwartship with four-by-twelves. Twin Isuzu diesels pushed its ungainly shape steadily along with anything but ease or grace. A boxy chicken-coop cabin aft was the builder's finishing touch. It is said that "the happiest days of a boat owner's life are the day he buys it and the day he sells it." Well, with interest rates over 20 percent and a ship's mortgage (backed by our island property) a few above prime, the honeymoon of ownership was short. With economic conditions driving coastal enterprises to virtual shutdown, we could count the list of barging prospects on one hand of a cross-eyed shingle sawyer.

Unfortunately, our run of bad decisions had not quite been exhausted. We concocted a solution that would satisfy all creditors and ensure our continued island ownership. Only fair to mention, there were no women involved in this planning session. We made a Hail Mary attempt to preserve

The *Inlet Vagabond,* a shipwreck waiting to happen.

the tatters of our wilderness dream. Scuttling our albatross sounded like a good idea at the time. We later learned it was a common story in those days. A fire or a shipwreck emerged as the two possibilities. Looking back, when tragedy looks like comedy, these seem appropriate because after four years, our plans, dreams and relationships all resembled a ship afire, stove-in, on a rockpile. Though the most plausible, fire was discarded as a bad idea. Surely some do-gooder would appear with a pump and promptly douse the flames before they could do a proper job of total destruction.

A question emerged: How many rocks does it take to sink a heavy wooden barge? First, we tested the buoyancy of a wood sample. We set about with tape measure, very sharp pencils and paper, and came up with a number of tonnes. After careful calculation and consideration for contingencies, we loaded the barge with enough rocks to send it straight to Davy Jones' Locker. After adding some for good measure, we still had plenty of rocks left in our heads. Even with a healthy surplus of rocks, the barge didn't quite sink. A sobering (no alcohol involved) sight it was, wallowing in the dark, listed over, decks awash, just the cabin, mast, and rails above water. I will spare you the torturous details of the outcome, culminating in total loss, bankruptcy, and relocation to Alert Bay. In short, everything sank but the barge. There followed many years of wondering, "Why didn't it sink? We did the math!"

Years later, in Marine College to obtain my Captain's Certificate, I studied Archimedes' principle of buoyancy: any object submerged or partially submerged in a fluid experiences an upward thrust equal to the weight of the fluid it displaces. My homework assignment had me muttering to myself about buoyancy and displacement all evening and through a fitful night. While shaving the next morning, I finally had the answer to my old question. We had not considered the buoyancy factor of the rocks once submerged! Of course, the commonsense explanation that some have offered is, "Well, things are lighter in water, eh?" I decided not to share with the class the story of our folly. So long before, chasing girls and other dubious pursuits were far more riveting than physics class, but I had finally come to appreciate the value of schooling.

Eventually, the psychodrama of small group isolation, financial struggle, marital upheaval, and breakdown of cohesive effort mirrored similar communal efforts of the era. Hindsight reads the chaos written clearly on the walls.

The Berry Island originals dwindled down to our little family—Vicki, me, and our darling Anna, just five years old. We left Berry Island, free of the struggles and problematic familial entanglements. We were relieved to focus on just our family's future. While hitching a boat ride, the skipper asked,

"Where do you want to go: Port McNeill, Alert Bay or Sointula?" After a short discussion on the aft deck where we mused about the vibrant cultural mix and friendly faces, I returned to the wheelhouse and replied, "Alert Bay." He turned, incredulous. "Are you sure?" I told him, "I'm not sure of much lately, but yeah, that is where we'll start." And we did.

We cautioned Anna to walk off the road, watch for cars and to hold our hand. She asked matter-of-factly, "Do cars bite?" She was really a wilderness kid, used to talk of bears, wolves and cougars. We came to love our new home. This funny, crazy, wonderful little island village welcomed us in, and we are part of it now. Our second daughter, Bridget, was born here, and both were raised here. They are not hot-house flowers. Our house is just a stone's throw from the saltchuck, overlooking Broughton Strait. We have a loving home that they and all the grandkids love to visit.

There has always been music in our family. Vicki has been in several groups, notably Alert Bay's own Broken Homes. Playing mostly old-time country songs, their mandate laughingly became, "Keeping heartbreak alive!" I have always written songs that basically chronicle my life. My same lovely guitar sailed on every boat and every motorcycle trip. My main shtick is coastal folk about various boats, crews, characters, and work that I have done and learned on this glorious coast. I'll keep writing and singing until I run out of time, because I know there will never be a shortage of material.

Stop by anytime and I'll play you a tune.

Karmsund

Howard Pattinson

The first fishboat I owned was built by a Norwegian-Canadian, "Hungry Olie," who had a reputation for pinching his pennies. I had worked for a season running fish collectors for Ocean Fisheries and had saved up $3,400 for a boat of my own. I planned on selling salmon directly to the public. My dad came to look the *Karmsund* over and, saint that he was, offered to match my funds. Then I went to the Fisherman's Credit Union and borrowed the rest, paying $19,000 for a beautiful schooner-sterned troller with a MD70 Volvo Penta engine.

It was the middle of winter, and I said to my brother, Alan, "We had better go clam digging with the boat, it's been sitting a while and we need to find out what's wrong with it." We headed off to Wyatt Bay on the north end of Quadra Island, where I had seen loads of butter clams the previous summer. When we got there and started looking, we realized someone had cleaned the clam beds out with a dredge. We scraped together only enough clams to pay for the fuel. And the engine's transmission started making grinding noises. We ran at idle throttle, with fingers crossed, to Heriot Bay, the closest road connection. About one hundred feet from the dock, the transmission gave out and we coasted in. We pulled the fish hold bulkhead off to get at the transmission. A logger walking the dock heard us in the hold discussing how to get the gear case off. He leaned down into the hatch and told us that there were jack bolt holes on each side of the gear casing, to just screw in the two bolts and the case would back off. "Thanks a lot!" We offered him some clams, and he laughed. "No, happy to help."

Alan took off hitchhiking to Vancouver to get his VW van to carry the three-hundred-pound monster transmission to a fix-it shop. In a couple of days, he was back. We used the dock winch to hoist the gear up to his van. Loaded up with the gear and clams (all three sacks of them), we headed to Vancouver. Everything went smoothly until we rounded the Fourth Avenue turn to Sixth Avenue at Birch. *Bang*, the side door of the van flew open, and the unsecured transmission flew out onto the road and smashed into a parking lot, which cracked the housing. We sheepishly rolled it back into the van and took it down to the Twin Disc repair shop near Cambie Street. Tom McBain, the service manager looked over the situation, saw the cracked

Offshore trolling in a fleet can be quite intense, watching for other boats. The vessel with its starboard pole to the beach has the right-of-way. Huge kelp islands that break free in storms can wreak havoc on the fishing gear, which is spread out by fifty-foot trolling poles set at 45 degrees to the horizon.

housing and guessed how broke we were. Tom was elderly, with the translucent appearance of a saint. He suggested we drive out to Nelson Brothers in Steveston and ask if they had a used Twin Disc on the shelf that we could have for fifty dollars. He could take both units apart and see if there were enough good pieces to rebuild our transmission. I looked at him, sure he was a saint. All my life I have tried to emulate him, helping young guys starting out.

When we got the boat back to Vancouver, we started to prepare it for the salmon season. The rusty rigging needed replacing, the hull painting, and each system working over. We made an appointment next month at the marine haul-out ways to copper paint the boat. Haul-out ways have a boat bridle on railroad tracks, which can pull a boat out at any stage of the tide. The cost was pricey, $150. We motored over to the wharf head to use the shore winch, but as we approached, about one hundred feet in front, we ran aground! In the middle of a busy harbour, we run aground! False Creek Sawmills had just shut down, and the sea bottom under its log booms had not been dredged. There we were, stuck fast, with the tide dropping. I paddled ashore to the sawmill site and was grabbing some lumber to shore up the boat when the owner of the sawmill yelled at us for stealing lumber. I pointed to our fast tipping boat, but he refused to change his mind. Definitely not a saint. I threw his lumber onto his feet. He called the cops.

Someone whistled from Arrow Transport across the pond. They dropped some beams into the water for us. With the help of a fast cutting swede saw we shored the boat upright, and watched the tide drop to a zero. The police

The crew at Arrow Transfer saved the *Karmsund* when we ran aground right off their wharf in False Creek. They threw down four-by-four beams to help us shore up the boat in a falling tide. Here the *Karmsund* shows off her spring paint and new wooden trolling poles, ready to head north to the fishing grounds.

came, and we could see them talking to the mill owner. They drove to the edge of the water, watched us scrambling around, and drove away, another couple of saints.

Finally, I said to brother Alan, "We might as well copper paint the boat, we have several hours until it floats." We scrubbed the bare hull, being careful not to knock the brace beams. Then we applied copper paint with the afternoon sun drying it nicely. Once the boat floated, we used the wharf winch to load the fishing gurdies and headed back to our float. An old-timer was there to help us tie up. "Just like Hungry Olie," he said, "too cheap to use the ways."

Our first salmon trip was up to Knight Inlet, where we used to collect gillnet fish. In the evening before the opening, we were tied up at Minstrel Island, trying to understand how to rig the trolling gear. An old-timer caught us inspecting his boats for hints. He offered to take us out for a couple of turns around the bay. He taught us how to work the gurdies, snaps, lines and lures. Another saint. The next morning, we caught one salmon. Alan kissed it on the nose and released it for good luck. Then we waited, nothing bit. The old-timer had said the previous evening that the fish were up the head of the inlet, so we ran seven hours up into God's country.

The steep snow-covered mountains held stunning views as we rounded every corner of the longest inlet on the BC coast. We put the lures in the water and the fish were biting like crazy. I said to Alan, "I bet if I put my thumb in the water, a salmon would bite it." You can still see the scar on my thumb!

La Sorella and Daytripper

Paul Bozenich for Nigel Hamilton

Nigel Hamilton (1946-2014)

Nearly six and a half feet tall, with long flowing black hair, David "Nigel" Hamilton's presence commanded attention. When he first landed in Sointula in 1973 he was in an entourage that included his girlfriend and two canine companions, an Afghan hound and a Malamute, along with a couple of fellow explorers. They had travelled from Powell River aboard the friends' boat, the *Kakua Lani*, a forty-foot ex-forestry cruiser, heading north in search of land to homestead. That effort had proved fruitless. By the time they reached Sointula, they all knew it was time to part ways. Nigel bounded off the boat and was back in short time to announce he had found a place to live as well as a job. Vintage Nigel.

Nigel Hamilton

With a somewhat aloof demeanour and British accent, Nigel stood apart from the US refugees and Canadian "back to the landers" who were flocking to the "Place of Harmony" in search of new horizons. Arriving in Canada from England in 1966, Nigel had worked at the pulp mill in Powell River and also laid bricks and mortar as he had been trained to do in his native city of York, England.

Nigel's voyage to Sointula from Powell River was his first taste of life on the sea and he was smitten. The first boat he bought ran pretty well the way he ran: straight forward, no turning back. It was a twenty-foot nameless plywood craft with a direct-drive gas engine. That engine, once started, had only one direction: forward.

Nigel on the *Sharon Marie* with skipper Len Pohto.

Nigel ran his life like that boat. Forward ho! Don't look back! His longtime friend, Murray Tanner, says, "He astonished me. Unlike most of us, when he set his mind to something, he did it. He got things done."

Top on Nigel's "to do" list was working. To this end he made himself handy doing masonry jobs, tree planting (a job not well suited to one built so high from the ground) and whatever odd jobs sprang up. His mainstay became fishing. In the seventies, he worked his way up from crewman on the smallest seine boat in the Sointula fleet, the *La Sorella*, to the high-liners, earning gratitude from his skippers and obeisance from his crew mates as he became recognized as the "deck boss" on any boat he worked.

Nigel earned his training wheels on the *La Sorella*, a converted troller built in Sointula by Laurie Jarvis, in one of the many boathouses that used to line the foreshore of the village. Jarvis had improvised the first power drum on a gillnetter but couldn't get a patent for it. He used the same technology to build some of the first power drums on seine boats, including the *La Sorella*. The first one he built was on the comically named *Who Cares*. (Imagine a skipper asking a deckhand holding binoculars what a boat on the horizon is. "*Who Cares*," replies the deckhand.) The *La Sorella* fished far from the madding crowd, using a shallow net that allowed it to fish spots in mainland inlets where deeper nets dared not set.

Victor Langvist remembers fishing with Nigel on both the *La Sorella* and the *Millionaires*, which Victor's dad and uncle co-skippered. You would be right to think that co-skippering a boat could lead to demonstrative disagreements. Victor says that Nigel and he would sometimes seek refuge behind the drum to share a doobie and a laugh. Crewing on the *Millionaires* was part fishing, part family reality show.

In the late summer of 1973, John Thorington had to go away on a family matter, leaving his wee gillnetter, the *Li'l Fisher*, in Nigel's charge.

Nigel, in turn, invited his friend Paul Bozenich to join in on this venture, yet another journey into the unknown for this pair. Previously, they had been novices in planting trees, moving houses, mining shake blocks, and razing an abandoned fish cannery together. "Why not," thought Paul, "what could go wrong?" Well, almost everything, as it turned out. The *Li'l Fisher* had its limitations. The boat was just eighteen feet long with only a 4.5 hp Seagull motor and had no drum, so only grit and biceps provided the power to bring in the net. No depth sounder... or radar... or radio... therefore fewer things to break down!

Nigel thought he had found the perfect setting for his first night ever gillnetting. He would drift along the sheltered shore between the lighthouse at Pulteney Point toward the mouth of Rough Bay and the Sointula Breakwater. In the middle of the night, they had lost sight of the lantern at the end of the net and lots of the corks had disappeared. Hopefully expecting to pull in a net weighted down with gilled fish, the pair instead pulled enough kelp and sticks aboard to nearly sink the *Li'l Fisher*. They spent most of the next day on a net float in the harbour. As a veteran gillnetter would say years later "you can tell someone not to do something, but when they try it and spend ten hours cleaning out their net the next day, they learn it."

After his misadventure in gillnetting, Nigel returned to working on seiners where his status as crew leader grew with the times. He worked his way through a succession of boats: the *Western Mist* (salmon), the *Island Rogue* (salmon); the *Island Breeze* (roe herring); the *Island Sun* (crabbing). It was a far cry from the days of banging his head on the galley entryway of the *La Sorella*.

Nigel's rise through the industry mirrored the expansion and evolution of the fishing industry of the late seventies and eighties. During the 1979 roe herring season, some buyers paid as high as $3,000 to $5,000 per tonne, almost five times more than what they had paid in 1976. The high-flying times spun the boatbuilding industry out of wooden and into steel, aluminum, and fibreglass boats. By the mid-eighties, the docks in Sointula more than doubled in size to accommodate the new flashy seine boats that were packed in like sardines during harbour time. It also rang the death knell for the once flourishing wooden boatbuilding industry in Sointula.

For a decade Nigel had to accommodate himself to other people's boats. Now he was ready to run his own. He had married the love of his life, Anita Sjoberg, and was a devoted husband and father. They purchased a thirty-seven-foot Deltaga fibreglass combination gillnetter/troller with a name befitting a displaced Brit: *Daytripper*. It had taken *sooo* long to find out that he could find his own way and chart his own course, with Anita as his first mate, except for the first year when she was saddled down on land with three young ones to care for.

Nigel did have one special deckhand aboard that first year. His father had come over from England and crewed with Nigel on the windy, rolling exposed north shore of Malcolm Island. Nigel got in trouble one night when he caught his net in the propeller. He radioed nearby fisher friends who quickly responded; one came to help out. Before he returned to England, Nigel's dad told Anita that his experience on the fishing grounds had assured him that he did not have to worry about his son due to the way he ran the boat and the camaraderie nearby if problems arose. When Nigel learned what his father said, Anita saw tears well up in his eyes, a rarity for this staunch Brit. His dad had been proud of him.

After his rookie season, Nigel recognized two needed changes to improve conditions on board. First, he would enlist Andy Anderson of Anderson Ways, from a third generation of boat builders in Sointula, to add six inches to the height of the *Daytripper*'s cabin. No more butting his head on his own boat. Second, he told Anita that he needed someone aboard who was svelte enough to reach in behind the cramped engine compartment in the *Daytripper* to change the fuel filter. She happened to fit the job description, and he had sorely missed her and the kids. Could they make this a family venture from then on? So, they did.

For the next decade, the Hamilton crew worked as a team, but like any team, you are not always controlling the puck. Nature and fortune have their fickle say in how things go. Even though it must have been hard for a person who put so much effort into plans only to have them altered by the course of events, Nigel had also developed such resilience that he could quickly alter his course and deal with the disruptions as they occurred.

Anita recalls several times when she had to rouse their children and have the survival suits close at hand. She shivered when she heard the voice of the notorious Captain Bob over the radio when they were gillnetting in Johnstone Strait at night. Captain Bob would plow through the scores of gillnets with his tug and barge as if he were dusting cobwebs. Once he passed so close they could see the cook pouring coffee in the galley's lights as the tug's engine roared deafeningly. All hands were on deck when Captain Bob came around.

On another occasion, the *Daytripper* had anchored in a bay just above the strong tidal channel of Seymour Narrows during a lightning storm. The family was settled in their bunks when the boat bounced on the bottom.

Homeward bound, *Eagle Spirit*, *Daytripper* and *Alta Loma*.

Nigel called for the trolling poles to be lowered as he radioed for help. Because of the lightning, radio transmission was poor. The boat was settling itself between boulders. Sointula gillnetter Vic Rhitamo responded to their mayday and secured a tow line, but the *Daytripper* was settling further with the falling tide. Fortunately, a passing cruise ship created enough of a swell to dislodge the *Daytripper*. Floating again, but not yet safe, as the rudder had been damaged and water was flooding into the stern. The steering made grinding noises and barely functioned as Nigel headed through the swirling waters of Seymour Narrows toward the safe harbour of Campbell River. With a Coast Guard rescue vessel alongside and the pumps whining, they made it to the docks in Campbell River and across to Quathiaski Cove for repairs the next day.

Nigel and Anita experienced many successful ventures as well. During one opening for chum (dog) salmon near Kitimat, their net was damaged by a floating tree, and they had to use an older, smaller-meshed sockeye net. They started catching so many heavy chum salmon that the corks were sinking. They remedied the situation by tying cylindrical bumpers along the net. Nigel told Anita that when the bumpers started to get "hard ons" it was time to pick the net. Anita said that by the end of the week, the net had sunk so much that corks were pretty useless as all the air had been pressed out of them.

As with all couples, it was not always calm waters in their relationship, says Anita. She recalls travelling through the Gulf of Georgia [Salish Sea] with a strong wind buffeting the *Daytripper* as it passed a sailboat off Texada Island. "What an idiot to be out in these seas," Nigel snorted. Just then, a big green curler hit Anita's side of the cabin, cracking the window, and the water came pouring in. Anita leapt out of her chair. "I'm fine, I'm fine," she exclaimed. "Forget about that!" Nigel retorted. "Save the TV!" The TV had no navigational function, but Nigel loved watching sporting events. Anita was not impressed with Nigel's order of priorities. The TV, after all, had never pulled a fish aboard.

To accommodate their growing family, Nigel convinced Anita that they should buy a second boat, the *Eagle Spirit*, which his older son, Tristan, (from a previous marriage) could run. Eventually their son Dustin ran it, with Anita aboard. They would fish nearby Nigel, who had their son Sid and daughter Amanda with him.

In the 1990s, the fishing income dwindled, and the family chose to sell their assets and move away from the once prosperous community of Sointula in search of opportunities elsewhere.

Nigel Hamilton is seated front and centre on the bow of the *Millionaires* on the cover of this book. That is appropriate: Nigel was the centre of attention when he arrived in Sointula, and he continued to be at the centre of many activities in his adopted community. Among the roles he assumed were leader (Akela) of the Scout pack, coach of both the Little League and the women's softball teams, and active member of the Lions' Club. He also built many a chimney and fireplace that warm residents in Sointula to this day. He had earned the respect of the community and the thanks of the many newcomers who were more tolerated and accepted because of Nigel's gung-ho enthusiasm in work and in service.

The writer would like to credit the contributions of Anita Hamilton, Murray Tanner, Andy Anderson, Greg Williams, Randy Williams, Victor Langvist, John Thorington, Dustin Hamilton, Wendy Poole, and other family and friends.

LCM

Paul Bozenich

In 1975, I "walked the docks" in Alert Bay on Cormorant Island for weeks looking for an opportunity to work on a seine boat. It was the peak of the sockeye run in the Johnstone Strait. My chances were better in Alert Bay than in neighbouring Sointula, on Malcolm Island, where I was homesteading in Mitchell Bay. Alert Bay had a much larger seine boat fleet, hence more boots to fill on Sunday mornings, when the stragglers left the docks to be on time when fishing opened at 1800 hours.

I came to Canada in late summer of 1971 as a war resister. To this day, I disdain the pejorative label of "draft dodger." When I arrived in British Columbia, I connected with Will and Heidi Soltau, friends from university days in Detroit. Will had fished on a seine boat that summer, which had docked in Sointula on the night of a dance. Enamored by the charms of the Finnish village, Will rented a house

Paul

the next morning. I helped his family move to Sointula from a farmhouse they were renting in Langley.

I had traded the ivy towers of universities for the cedar towers of the rain forests. Finding a logging job on Malcolm Island, I helped to drag those once towering cedars out of their lodgings. For decades afterwards, I helped to plant and protect new cedar seedlings. A broken wheel is hard to set straight again, but I try.

By 1975, I was mostly a bachelor working on my master's in animal husbandry. My five-acre homestead at times had goats, sheep, chickens and ducks wandering about looking for holes in the fencing so they could annoy my neighbours—I learned bad fences make bad neighbours. Meanwhile, many of my fellow coastal newcomers had ventured into commercial fishing. They would return from their fishing trips with tales of adventure and fortune to be had. I wanted a piece of that action! Having worked with these novice seafarers at other pursuits, I thought, "If they can do it, so can I."

Finding a job on a seiner had not been easy. On this particular morning though, my luck changed. I encountered a lean, angular man on an old wooden black and white seine boat with the letters *LCM* on her bow. He identified himself as Bob and he spoke with an accent I identified as Yugoslav, having had grandparents who all immigrated to America from the "old country." Bob actually asked *me* if I was looking for a job. "Yes."

"You work on seine boat before?"

"No."

"That okay.... You be cook."

And Bingo! I was a seiner!

Bob said he needed to run some errands and bounded off, leaving me in sole charge of his vessel. What a stroke of luck! As cook, a role I felt capable of filling, I would be able to break in by observing the crew at work. It was midseason and they should be in good form. *Where was the rest of this well-oiled team?* I wondered. Before long I found out. A slight, long-haired bearded man named Peter hopped aboard.

"How is Bob to work for?" I was keen to know.

"Don't know, I just got hired."

"What's your job?"

"Skiff man."

"Have you seined before?"

"No."

Soon after, a broadly built man swung himself onto the *LCM*'s deck.

"What's this skipper like to work for?"

"Dunno. Just got on," said George in a speech as short-clipped as his hair. "Bin workin' in the woods... strike... laid off."

"Bummer. Have you seined before?"

"Never, but I've run cats and skidders so's I'm the drum man, he tells me."

A shadow was starting to fall across my shiny dream for a prosperous week of fishing.

Our final crew member was next to board. Dave told us that he had been working with Bob for two openings as the beach or tie-up man. In a strong tide, the one-and-a-half-inch rope holding the end of the net to a tree or boulder on shore goes off like a shotgun blast when released. Not a job for the faint-hearted, but Dave seemed the stalwart sort. Dave told us he had made no money so far, but he stayed on because he was being fed and bedded. When he was asked what Bob was like to work for, he chuckled. "You'll see."

Bob returned with a cart of provisions and quickly fired up the engine. We were steaming off... before anyone could change their mind. After stowing the food, I climbed up to the bridge, the open-air steering station above the wheelhouse. I learned that Bob (his anglicized name) came from the Dalmatian coast of former Yugoslavia, where some of my ancestors lived. He was disappointed that the only Yugoslav I understood were words I learned from my elders as a child. They translated into warnings like "Don't," "Shut up," "Hurry up," "Never mind," along with a few colourful curses. All useful phrases to know as the week progressed.

Bob was in an ebullient mood as the *LCM* cruised down the Johnstone Strait on a bright, breezy afternoon. Seine boats were lining up at the favoured spots on the "fishier" side of the Strait. Bob was trying to get me to join in with him as he belted out Dalmatian folk songs.

I asked him how long he had been running the boat. "Yust this year. I trade my gillnetter, the *Dubrovnik* for this," he boasted. *So, he is nearly as green as the rest of us,* I thought. *Oh, oh.*

Bob radioed in for a turn in a lineup and we anchored. The net was splayed out on the stern, and it was hard for me to imagine how it was going to rearrange itself and bring in fish for our holds.

At 1800 hours calls of "Let her go!" rang out and the skiffs headed to shore. Boats that were ahead of us in the lineup completed their sets, pulling up impressive "bags" of salmon. After several hours it was our turn, our chance to shine.

The beach crew was poised for action in our skiff at the stern of the boat. George was poised to strike the pelican hook to release the skiff from the boat. Dave was ready to plunge the sea anchor into the chuck when the skiff was released, enabling the net to be pulled off the mothership. When Bob yelled, "Let her go," Dave let the sea anchor go, but George swung and missed on his first two attempts to release the skiff. The net was taking off but not the skiff. Third time lucky and the skiff was finally released, but we were well past the tie-up tree. The crew did not have enough rope to reach anything to tie to. As a result, our net drifted along the beach instead of holding taut to it, diminishing our chances of rounding up schools of fish.

At least we got the net back and wound on the drum. Mostly pink salmon, not the cleverest of fish, were in the bag we pulled aboard. The swift and evasive sockeye continued to outwit us as the week progressed.

Myrriah, the leader of the herd. My choice in goats was better than my choice in boats.

It was a learning experience, I kept telling myself. By the end of the week, I was introduced to a glossary of terms for the mishaps that befell us: rollups, lead line over, spilling the rings, back hauling, backlashes, and the accompanying backaches. My main responsibility was coiling the purse line on deck as I winched it in. After experiencing several frustrations and near castrations, I started calling it the curse line.

Our most serious mishap was when we got our net wrapped around our propeller, stalling the engine and rendering us helpless. With darkness setting in, a compatriot of Bob's slowly towed us to a dock in Growler Cove with our net dragging behind and Bob on the bridge yelling at our rescuer to "go faster" between various Croatian curses. The next morning, a diver freed the net. We made a rudimentary patch and headed back to the fishing grounds, as we had heard that the fishery had been extended for two more days and many of the seiners were loading up.

I was beginning to miss my goats.

Bob reckoned that the clutch control on the bridge was allowing the boat to slip into reverse and entangle the net. To prevent this, Bob took me into the fish hold and uncovered the shaft log, exposing the propeller shaft. He showed me how to attach two large pipe wrenches on either side of the shaft and wedge them against the wooden sides of the surrounding box. After this, every time we started to drum the net, I had to jump into the hold and attach the wrenches.

Back on the grounds, we were on our own at any spot that Bob chose. Perhaps word had gone out that our mishaps were causing delays to boats following us in the lineup, and the skippers were avoiding getting behind the *LCM*. At the change of the tide, we were drumming in our net and drifting perilously close to shore, with no other boat around to tow us off. "Whip 'er in," commanded Bob as he hustled up the ladder to the bridge. As soon as the net was aboard, the *LCM* lurched away from the shore, unleashing a racket of noise from the fish hold: the sound of splintering wood. The pipe wrenches had not been released and were splintering the wood encasing the shaft.

I climbed up to the bridge to make a damage report. Luckily, the few fish in the hold were spared. I also informed Bob that I was quitting as of NOW, but I would continue to cook meals and help out on deck. I would not take a crew share, if we were even to earn one, and I would not be fishing on the *LCM* after this trip. And, no, I wouldn't be singing on the bridge with him.

With a prized pot plant, "working gauge," vintage Mitchell Bay, circa 1974.

Bob surprised me by taking this news in stride, and it freed me to gain a new perspective. In the evenings I felt deserving enough to indulge in my small stash of homegrown marijuana. Having quit the boat, I was immune to being fired.

In a movie script, the *LCM* would make a huge catch of sockeye just before closing time. This is not what happened. Fishing is a fluky endeavour, but good luck usually follows those prepared for it. The *LCM* was not. After four days, the fishing, mercifully, ended.

We delivered our meager catch to a packer and Bob chose to tie up at the docks in Sointula. He figured he could find replacements for myself and George, who was gratefully heading back to work in the woods. Dave and Peter decided to stay for the free bed and board… and the next round of punishment.

We sat around the galley in a relaxed atmosphere for once. Although the trip was unrewarding, at least we were exiting from it unscathed. We mused about the name of the boat. Nobody knew what *LCM* stood for, but we agreed that after the week we had we would remember it as the Larry, Curly & Moe.

Bob said he had noticed the funny smell from that stuff I was smoking. He said he had never smoked pot. Could he try some? I was down to my last doobie, so I lit it up and passed it to Bob. He took the briefest of puffs on it, and then threw it out of the galley window and into the chuck. My jaw dropped! "Marijuana, I don't see what the big deal is," he proclaimed, much to my chagrin.

Later that week, a friend told me Bob had been telling all who cared to listen that he had a poor fishing week because the cook, a hippie from Mitchell Bay, had put marijuana into the food.

After this experience, I did not return to fishing until 1978, after I had started practising human husbandry. I was fortunate to have crewed with some of the many distinguished skippers out of Sointula. I packed herring and salmon on Michael Hawkes' packer, the *Gallant Girl*, and ran it for two seasons when Michael returned to England. My fishing experience extended to Alaska where I crewed on a gillnetter in Bristol Bay and on a freezer troller out of Sitka.

Peter quit the *LCM* during the next opening in a unique way. He handed his oars over to Dave after Dave had tied to the shore. Peter stayed alone at the tie-up spot until he found another beach crew willing to take him to their boat.

I never saw Dave or George on the fishing grounds again.

I heard that Bob died of a heart attack the next year. He was very excitable.

The *LCM* went to its watery grave rounding the north end of Vancouver Island in the late seventies.

Li'l Fisher and VO

John Thorington

In June 1970, the day after writing my last high school exam, I boarded a train to Vancouver and left Orillia, Ontario, behind. I remember being blown away by the Rocky Mountains. From Vancouver, I caught a bus to Powell River, where a bunch of guys from Orillia were already living. For a couple of months, I roomed with some of the guys that I'd gone to school with until I found a little place to rent on Cranberry Lake. In early August, I got a "Dear John" letter from my on-and-off girlfriend from high school. By my nineteenth birthday in December, I was married, had a job at the mill, and was the father of a beautiful baby girl.

Living in Powell River was a real eye-opener. The beauty of the rugged West Coast with its majestic mountains and clear blue ocean was so different from central Ontario. I was falling in love with the West Coast. Our marriage only lasted about a year and a half, and she went back to Ontario with

A common Sointula fisherman's white hat.

Putting up the mast on the *Li'l Fisher* at the Sointula dock, tied under the Norpac barge, with my young daughter supervising.

our daughter. In 1973, I went with a friend to Sointula to visit another friend, Nigel Hamilton, who we knew from Powell River. In those days, the ferry left from Kelsey Bay mid-afternoon, stopping in Beaver Cove, Alert Bay and then spending the night in Sointula. The following morning the ferry would make the return trip to Kelsey Bay. There was often a movie played on a big screen during the ferry ride.

We found Nigel's place a few blocks from the ferry that evening. The following morning Nigel got his boat and picked us up in front of his house. His house became known as the Graveyard House because it was right beside the graveyard. Quite a few young people came through that house in those years. Nigel and his partner, Sue, and their dogs, took us to Pulteney Point where we spent three or four days helping and hanging out with two young families who were homesteading on a piece of land that went across the peninsula of land behind the Pulteney Point lighthouse. These folks, Will and Heidi Soltau and Kit and Stephanie Eakle, had young children. I remember being so impressed by their hard work carving out an existence in this very remote place. I was so taken by the experience that I thought this would be a good place to relocate. So, without really seeing the town of Sointula, I went back to Powell River, packed up all my possessions, headed back to Malcolm Island and moved in with Nigel and Sue.

At first not everyone in Sointula was overly welcoming to a long-haired hippie type moving into their quiet village. You could hardly blame them for being cautious as the community was mostly made up of old Finnish families that had settled Malcolm Island in the early 1900s. At one time, the neighbours on either side of us included older women who didn't speak any English, only Finnish. I think the villagers assumed that if you were new and had long hair, you were probably an American war resister. The more involved you became in the community, the more accepted you became. Folks were really so helpful and willing to share their knowledge if you showed a keen interest. That was what I found after buying the *Li'l Fisher* and a truck that came with the contract to haul the freight from the weekly barge to the Co-op Store. Seaspan operated a weekly scheduled run from Vancouver that served remote communities up and down the coast and brought everything and anything.

The *Li'l Fisher* was an eighteen-foot flat-bottomed plywood boat with a square bow and a very small cabin that was only about four feet tall. It was built in a front yard in Sointula by a mother and her teenaged son so they could fish right in front of Sointula. The son wasn't old enough to fish on his own. I bought it in the fall, and it sank a couple of times, so I towed it to the Graveyard House and pulled it into the boatshed on the property. Come spring the twelve-horsepower gas engine that powered the drum had seized up, so I removed the drum and the engine and set it up to haul by hand. (I may have been the last fisherman to gillnet by hand—by choice.) I bought an English-made outboard motor, a British Seagull 4.5 hp from Alert Bay, and started the sockeye season as green as they get. I fished right in front of Sointula with a short net—about 130 fathoms instead of 200 fathoms. There were so many things that went wrong but, luckily, I learned from most of them. I remember the time I drifted past the graveyard and almost onto the reef because the tide was running so hard. While fighting the tide on the way back, there were a handful of people burying a loved one in the cemetery. There I was, motoring by at a snail's pace with the Seagull just screaming. I was so embarrassed. Several times I blocked the dock where the ferry was to land. The skipper would sit there blowing his horn and there was not a lot that I could do quickly. That spot in front of the dock was the best gillnetting spot on the whole drift.

My favourite memory of the *Li'l Fisher* was a dark set I made by John's farm and caught eighty-eight large Adams River sockeye. A dark set is made just before the sun goes down, one of the best times because the fish can't see the net, same goes for the opposite, the morning set as the light starts to change. I was pitching the fish into the fish box on the deck and the sides blew. There were fish everywhere. I had to go and tie up to the Norpac barge for the night and deliver in the morning.

During that first year with the *Li'l Fisher* my family situation changed when my first wife back in Ontario passed away from cancer. So, with some serious convincing on my part as no one thought that I should be bringing up a child on my own, I brought my daughter, Nicole, back to BC. I really wanted to try to make a go of the life I had started. I was so young and undoubtedly naive. I said to myself, "Ontario will always be there," and it still is! At the time I was living in small A-frame cabin with no power or water. We ended up living in the Graveyard House after Nigel and Sue bought some property out Kaleva, a road that followed the south shore of the island.

The next year, 1975, there was a strike of shoreworkers and fishermen that lasted for four weeks, mid-July to mid-August. I ended up getting a job on a seine boat, the *Millionaires*, for the rest of the season. It was very interesting to say the least and I did learn some useful things.

I met some very interesting people in Sointula. Perhaps the most interesting was a man named Walter Siider, who had grown up as a pioneer on the island. He told stories of rowing himself and his sister to school from the farm at a time before there were roads on the island. Through that friendship, I bought a little twelve-by-twenty-four-foot house on skids that was on his land next to his trailer at the head of Rough Bay. We strapped a trailer axle under the skids and picked the front end up with a skidder and towed the house through town to Nigel's land. I helped to move a few houses around the island. It was commonplace to buy a house, tow it onto a float with a cat, and tow the float with a boat to a different piece of property and do the reverse, tow it off onto its new home. It was hard, dangerous work, especially moving the logs that are used as rollers to move the house on the rocky beaches. I think it was one of the worst things I did for my back. It was those kinds of projects that brought the community together to help one another and accomplish things that you couldn't do on your own.

Shortly after moving the house, I met my second wife. The following year we bought a lot in town in Rough Bay and moved the house back to within blocks of where it was originally. We had two more daughters, Ona in 1976 and Laurel in 1979. I built a couple of additions on the little house and the original structure became the kitchen and dining room.

The year after that short season with the *Millionaires*, I got a job with Robert Belveal and fished for two seasons with him. Robert was a gentle giant of a man with a huge heart and a fabulous sense of humour. I'll never forget his morning ritual getting up before the crack of dawn, making a big pot of coffee and a tall stack of toast, and yelling down the fo'c'sle: "Let go of your cocks and pull up your socks, there's daylight in the swamp." Waking up every morning to this announcement always put a smile on my face no matter how tired I was. It still does. I have thought of Robert as my Sointula dad since then. I learned a lot from Robert in those years and afterwards. While we were seining, I would be asking him questions about what the gillnetters were doing and why. Later on, we fished side by each longlining for halibut and gillnetting salmon after Robert left seining.

We were lucky in the seventies as there were opportunities to make money if you were willing to work. Tree planting became a good fill-in job in the off-season, and I got to see a bit of the BC interior. There was also work in the boat shop and other odd jobs. It was 1975 or 1976 when I got my first job herring fishing. In those days there were two nets allowed per licence and we had two licences so four nets in the water most of the time. We would fish the west coast, then the central coast and then the north coast. Those early years we shook the nets by hand, had no power anything so the lights at night were Coleman lanterns mounted on aluminum stands fore and aft in the punt. The three of us shook up to one hundred tonnes a season. You knew the meaning of "puckered asshole" after a season.

In 1978, I bought the *VO*, a thirty-two-foot double-ender gillnet boat, from the same man who had sold the *Li'l Fisher* to me. I started to learn a lot fast about fishing and maintenance, engine and mechanics, navigation and, of course, net mending, which I needed to do regularly. In those years I mostly fished Johnstone Strait, the north shore of Malcolm Island, and Smith Inlet. The following year I put on gurdies, so now there was trolling to fill in the time when there wasn't any gillnetting. Fishing in Smith Inlet brings back some of my fondest memories of fishing off steep beaches. Smith Inlet sockeye are nice big fish and I swear they hit the net harder than any other fish. I loved it. One year they opened what they called the lake, but was actually Wyclees Lagoon, so up the river I went and fished for a week in the lake, no tide. It was a bit of a navigational nightmare getting up there and back out again but what an experience.

I think in the seventies we came to Malcolm Island with our own new ideals. The Vietnam war was going on and peace and love was definitely our generation's mantra. We were a different generation than our parents, but I think we carried some of our parents' values with us still. My choices and, more often than not, the opportunities that came around from those, led me down a path of employment where I learned carpentry, plumbing, basic wiring, house building, and how to fix most things wooden. It didn't come

On the *VO*, getting ready to set the salmon net somewhere in Area 12 around Johnstone Strait.

naturally to me, but I even learned how to do basic mechanics, enough to keep the boat running. I have to say that being a fisherman throughout the seventies and learning carpentry have taught me skills that I still use today. As well, I think I learned as much, if not more, about life by being a parent and hopefully learning from past mistakes. And I am grateful to the many people that helped me along the way.

Looking back, the ideals that I had when I came to BC are still somewhat in line with my ideals of today. I feel very fortunate that I was born in this country to good parents and had the opportunities I had. Those experiences in the seventies led to bigger and better things. In the eighties, I bought the *Malcolm Isle,* which had a halibut licence as well as a salmon licence. Halibut fishing was great. I never knew what may come up on the next hook: an octopus, or a wolf eel, or a cod with something else eating it.

We moved to the Comox Valley in the late eighties, and I fished out of there into the early nineties. Now my boating experiences are back to where I started as a Boy Scout: canoeing. I met one of the *Dancing in Gumboots* girls, Sue Wheeler, in 1996, and we enjoy retirement together with our kids and nine grandkids.

A big thank you goes out to everyone along the way.

Millionaires

Rick James

Back in the early seventies, when I was a long-haired hippie renting an old shack out in the Happy Valley behind Courtenay, I would often hitchhike to Victoria to visit my family and hang out with some of my old "tune in, turn on, drop out" buds once again. Then, sometime in 1973, I met up with one of the old gang, Suzelle. While catching up with each other, she told me that she was living in Sointula, which she found to be one "perfect paradise" situated up off the north end of the Island. Upon hearing this, I was keen to check it out for myself, especially after learning that its original settlers were

On Malcolm Island I was known as "Rick the Hippie."

so much like us hippie types, being utopian dreamers. These were Finnish immigrants who had secured a large parcel of land on Malcolm Island in the early 1900s and set out to escape capitalist overlords by creating their own independent socialist commune.

Once I was there and crashing in the little cabin Suzelle was renting, I spent some time wandering around Malcolm Island's gorgeous landscape and the village of Sointula, situated right above the beach looking out across the water to Vancouver Island. I fell in love with the small community and moved up there the following year, 1974. Once there, I rented a lovely old pioneer log cabin which was built back in the early 1900s, where I could look out a large window while eating and watch the tide moving in and out over Rough Bay's beautiful tidal flats. I lived there until finally having to move out in 1985.

Even though I was comfortably settled in on the island, I still needed a job to pay the rent and buy groceries, as well as a bottle of scotch, which I so loved to drink at the time. I became good friends with some of the other peace-loving characters, eager back-to-the-landers, along with a few Vietnam war draft dodgers and deserters who had escaped across the border and made their way onto the island. We were all eager to earn a living, and a group of us decided to form our own tree planting venture, Treesing Reforestation Cooperative. Although it provided us all with a half decent income, there were far better ways to earn a good dollar, with opportunities coming from living close to the water. Inside the Rough Bay breakwater many trollers, gillnetters, draggers and seiners were tied up. Back then, throughout the seventies, the net boats were reaping fabulous returns, especially harvesting Fraser River sockeye passing through Johnstone Strait in the summer.

Since there was such a large fleet tied up in the Bay, there were two fish buying stations, Millerds and Norpac, with freezers set up on barges tied up next to the floats. It was here that I made my entry into the fabulous commercial fishing industry. After introducing myself to the guy running Norpac, he hired me to help him unload boats delivering their catches and carry the fish into the freezer. I soon began considering

Weekend net mending for the crews of seine boats *Star Tania* and *Maple Leaf C*, Sointula, July 1982. Photo Rick James

The *Millionaires* headed out for an opening with its hippie crew aboard, summer of 1975. Photo Rick James

running down a far better opportunity working in the industry.

At that time there were around fifteen seiners fishing out of Sointula and I was hoping that I'd be able to land a good paying job working on one. I was fortunate since back then they often found themselves short a crewman and were having a hard time finding guys. Malcolm Island's population was only around seven hundred people or so back then. Besides that, there were so many other well-paying jobs available: running your own troller or gillnetter, working in one of the town's boatyards, or off and away in a logging camp somewhere along the coast. So "Rick the Hippie," as I soon became known around town, eventually found work crewing on a local purse seiner. I started working out on deck, running the purse line winch, and finally got the opportunity to run the skiff. I absolutely loved it, just sitting out at the end of the net after making a set. It was so danged quiet and peaceful back when the skiffs were still powered by oars and not by outboard engines. Once I was behind the oars in an aluminum skiff, I got to listen to the very chatty local killer whale pod, who were in Johnstone Strait with us, catching sockeye to fill their bellies.

The first seiner I crewed on was the *Millionaires*, owned by two brothers who were hiring many a hippie off the dock in the mid-seventies. Nearly all of

them only lasted three weeks at most before jumping ship, since all the screaming and yelling going on back and forth between the two brothers drove them
crazy. "… Don't just stand there for fug sakes!! Grab the god-damned purse
line!! And start pursin' or were gonna lose 'em all!!" was common.

Regardless of this obnoxious behaviour, the first week I crewed on the
Millionaires, the owners made a good call. They headed over to the entrance
to Knight Inlet since they figured there would be a good run of humpies
(pink salmon) returning there. And they were right. We made one big haul.
On delivering our catch to Norpac, we crew members reaped a $1,200 share
each, which was big bucks back in those days. On the next opening a week
or two later we headed out into Blackfish Sound, which lies off the east end
of Malcolm Island. Salmon returning to the Fraser River to spawn, if they
don't go down the outside of Vancouver Island, choose to run down through
the inside waters down into Queen Charlotte Strait into Blackfish Sound
and then into Johnstone Strait. That is a faster and easier route to the Fraser
since the incoming tide would flood down the Strait like a river into the Gulf
of Georgia.

Once we were out there, Leslie, who was on top of the cabin behind the
wheel, figured we'd arrived at the perfect spot to make our first set and yelled
out, "Get ready guys, we's are gonna drop her here right off Swanson [Is-
land]." But then Dave yelled back up from the deck at him, "What the hell?!
We don't wanna set here, all the gol-danged schools are gonna be sittin' off
of Hanson [Island] fer fug sakes!" And it wasn't just us guys working on deck
having to listen to all this incredibly loud and obnoxious screaming, so did
all the other seiners working Blackfish Sound waters. Some of the guys told
us once we were back ashore that they actually found it most entertaining
listening to all that madness rolling across the water. Regardless of so many
of us newcomers having put up with this behaviour, we are indeed indebted
to the brothers for providing us an entry into the commercial fishing industry in its heyday.

Enough was enough, so I finally quit after three weeks of putting up
with all that madness, but luckily was able to sign on the Canfisco (Canadian
Fishing Company) seiner *Cape Ross* soon afterwards. It proved to be a good
call since it was being run by Lorrie Stauffer, a most pleasant gentleman
living in Sointula, who had taken charge in 1976. He and his father and
brothers, who were fishing out of Alert Bay, were some of the most skilled
net menders on the coast. But when he set out to teach me how to mend,
he was somewhat perturbed watching me trying to follow his directions. It
was challenging for me—he was somewhat hard to follow, being so agile and

fast working a needle. And he found teaching me frustrating, since I was left-handed—my needle and twine were directed backwards in the opposite direction. Still, I was finally able to catch on.

In 1980, Lorrie was running the BC Packers' seiner *Chief Tapeet*, which I crewed on for the next couple of years. The most rewarding sites for us to make sets were just off Blinkhorn Peninsula, which is a short distance from Telegraph Cove at the entrance to Johnstone Strait or Robson Bight a little ways farther down in the Strait. Orcas have their rubbing spot here, just around the corner from the bight. One day we made a beach set on the point at the top end of the bight and were sitting there on the rocks when some orcas came rolling along, heading out of the bight and swimming directly toward the open net. *Jeez Murphy!* I thought. *Hey, they're going to get themselves entangled in it!* But they dove down just a few feet away, disappeared, and then a couple of seconds later rose to the surface on the inside of the set to continue on their way, headed toward Blinkhorn.

Man, oh man! Some of the catches we made off those spots! What proved particularly rewarding was when a bag was brought in close to the stern rollers and was too overloaded with fish to be drummed up. So, we had to bring the net alongside and brail them all up onto deck to be tossed down into the hold. Yes indeed, it was one great experience working with Lorrie in those early years, especially after we'd deliver our catch over in Alert Bay, then run through our net and do some mending if needed in the BC Packers net loft. Once done for the day, we'd head off up the road to the funky old Nimpkish Hotel for a beer or two or three or perhaps more. The Nimpkish was a very pleasant old pub to sit and relax in. It sat out on a pier and was wrapped around with windows where we could look across Broughton Strait up into the Nimpkish valley and river delta. Still, I finally decided to call it quits with Lorrie after he was asked to run the seiner *BC Girl*. I decided to move on since word around the docks was that the boat was in bad shape or owned by a difficult guy to work for.

It didn't take long for me to land another job aboard the seiner *Bligh Island* run by another easy-to-work-for Sointula guy, Larry Schoberg. But still, I ended up jumping ship in Vancouver after delivering our load. For a change, we had tried fishing the open Pacific waters outside off Vancouver Island. As usual, a mild westerly wind was blowing, and a swell was running. We ended up rolling around in the swell. I was tending the purse line after we'd made a set off the entrance to Port Renfrew, when all the lead line's rings flew off the hairpin which shot off like a rocket on its line and came flying back only a couple of inches away from my head. Man, oh man, I was

Once done for the day, we'd head off up the road to the funky old Nimpkish Hotel for a beer or two or three or perhaps more.

majorly traumatized. If it had smacked me in the head, it would have been lights out for me.

After walking away from the boat after this nasty experience, I continued working on the water as a skiffman, after lucking out by being taken on by another pleasant guy, Robert Belveal, who was running Ocean Fisheries' seiner *Hard Times.* Those were good years since Robert was mostly an easy-going guy, even if he still did scream at us the odd time if we weren't quite on the ball and were screwing up. The overriding rule of working on fishboats is "Move it or lose it!" Still, after enjoying an incredible and particularly rewarding adventure working out in Johnstone Strait through those years netting sockeye along with coho, humpies, and dog salmon up and down the coast, I finally called it quits at the end of the 1986 season. The heyday of net fishing was over. Now a weekly opening was only for a couple of days rather than three or four like it was back when we were making a killing.

Looking back, all those years provided a golden opportunity for those of us who had moved to Sointula, not only because we could earn a big dollar working out on the water, but also because we were able to get along so well with the sons and daughters of the original utopian dreamer pioneers. In a sense, I was even to have some step-parents while living there. I used to deliver dog (chum) salmon to Ray (Tauno) Salo, who would smoke them in his backyard overlooking the waterfront. He enjoyed me dropping by so he could catch up on all that was going on out on the water. Ted (Teuvo) and Janet Tanner loved babysitting my dog, Ruba, as did the Salos, while I was away fishing. And Granny Jarvis (Helmi Jarvelainen), whom I had done gardening for when I first arrived. Her deceased husband Laurie had designed and built the very first gillnet drum sometime around 1931. Granny would have me in for lunch while carrying on a nice chat so she could check up on how I was doing and was getting by.

Sointula was an ideal place, both economically and socially, to be living in and working out of through the seventies into the eighties. Indeed, after the federal government carried out a national survey sometime mid-decade of per capita income, the small Malcolm Island village was right up there at the top of the list. Rick the Hippie garnered one good dollar after another while working on seiners back when there were fabulous returns of Fraser River sockeye passing through local waters. Then, with my sharing my tales of this fabulous experience, one friend replied, "Oh I get it. So, you started out with *Millionaires* earning big bucks but when *Hard Times* finally came along you decided it was time to call it quits."

Myrtle V

Tom Pearson

After forty years of commercial fishing, I often think how lucky I was to have wound up doing it for a living. I grew up in a small town in Ontario called Strathroy. I came west to Banff for most of the seventies and met many like-minded people who were active, wanted to ski, play hockey and enjoy life. After ski trips to the coast and Vancouver Island, I knew BC was where I wanted to be.

Tied up at Fairview 2 in Rupert. Waiting for the weather to get back out fishing.

One of my ski buddies, Bob Nagge, had followed his girl-friend to Prince Rupert, where she worked at the Prince Rupert Fishermen's Co-op for the herring season. He got a job deckhanding on the *Summer Wind* with Ken Erikson for the salmon troll season. He eventually bought his own troller, the *Shar-bon*, and I came out to fish with him. Both of us thought how great it was to work hard for four or five months a year and have the rest of the year off to ski and travel.

I started deckhanding in 1978 and bought my own boat in 1983. The Eriksons, who were third generation fishermen, helped me pick out a forty-two-foot wooden troller called the *Myrtle V*. The jump from deckhanding to running my own boat was huge. I knew how to run the gear and clean and ice fish, but there are so many decisions to make when you are the skipper. I think the first year of starting any business is maybe the most difficult: some make it, and some don't. I was fortunate enough to make it, with the support of my friend Bob on the *Shar-Bon*, and the Erikson family.

My story is about a halibut trip that we made during the derby days in the early eighties, an opening in April. We were in Rupert at the dock at the Ocean Fisheries plant getting ready, busy winding the ground line on, sharpening hooks, getting flagpoles and anchors on. Always lots to do. My crew

Myrtle V anchored in Pruth Bay near Hakai Pass. On our way home, but time to see some beautiful beaches.

included Kendal Smith, Mike Prescott and Wally Morgan, the in-breaker, from Kitwanga.

A run-down, well-known Rupert boat came and tied to us and within minutes Mike told me he had just seen a rat jump on board. We had spare ground and buoy lines lashed down along the wheelhouse, and totes of hooks and snaps along with the drum on the back deck—lots of places for a rat to hide. We were so busy that I soon forgot about it. We took ice and some bait and ran down to Fairview to get away from the commotion at Ocean.

Kendal's wife, Donna, and my friend Maureen came down that evening with a pie and some baking for our trip. We had a couple of beers and left Rupert at midnight, headed for Haida Gwaii. I was at the wheel early that morning as we headed out Edye Passage and started to cross the Hecate Strait. Suddenly, I saw the rat on the foredeck! I had totally forgotten about the rat! This wasn't a cute, little field rat but a big, greasy Rupert rat. I grabbed a deck brush to club it, but it quickly disappeared into the anchor winch. I ran

Decks awash. Off Rose Spit and heading to Rupert to deliver some salmon. Blowing about 15-20 westerly.

back and got the kettle off the stove. I thought that if I poured hot water on the winch and chain, it would come out, which did not work. We didn't see it for a while. Occasionally, it would come out and be on the foredeck but would disappear before we could get to it. I usually had a 410 on board and would have been blasting away, but I had no gun this trip.

We got to the bait pond in Selwyn Inlet and got our fresh herring. After anchoring up we got ready for the noon opening on the following day. It was important that the rat didn't get into the cabin or fo'c'sle, so we closed the cabin door and all the windows. It was soon so hot that I turned off the stove.

It was pretty uncomfortable for us all, and I thought it would be a tough opening day if we didn't get a good sleep. Later, I could hear the rat tinkling around in the hooks tote and eventually finding its way to a garbage bag hanging from a cleat on the mast. *This might be my chance!* I thought. I whispered to the boys in the fo'c'sle to come up and turn on the deck lights as soon as I jumped out on deck. Dressed in my undies, gumboots and a pair of heavy icing gloves, I jumped and grabbed the garbage bag and heaved it overboard. The bag hit the back stays and fell back on deck. I thought, *Oh shit*, but then saw the rat cartwheeling over the side. I could see its beady, red eyes shining in the deck lights. It swam back to the boat but was impossible to see under the guard. I quickly grabbed a long halibut gaff and rubbed it back and forth along the waterline. Three times I dislodged it and tried to gaff it. The rat knew it was in trouble. Maybe I got it with the gaff, or it finally tired, but the tide eventually took it away. The bright, red eyes disappeared behind us much to our great relief. I restarted the stove and opened the windows and fo'c'sle hatch cover and we all got a good sleep. I thought that night that everyone should have a garbage bag on board as a rat trap!

We had good fishing and delivered to the *Norqueen* behind Reef Island and got fresh bait and ice every couple of nights. Hard work and not a lot of sleep. When the opening was over, we ran to Rupert and delivered at Ocean Fish. We coiled some of the gear off, showered up and headed uptown.

It was a night at the Belmont that I fondly remember. The northern halibut fleet was in town, and we were all ready to let off some steam. There were two big screens playing the Stanley Cup playoffs with a stripper dancing in between. I thought I had died and gone to heaven! All that hard work, the aches and pains from long days and little sleep and now here we all were, having so much fun! I will always be proud and thankful that I fished during those halibut derby days. It was such a hard, tough fishery but so memorable and rewarding.

After halibut, we would run back down to Comox to get hauled out, paint the boat and get ready for salmon trolling. We would be back up in Rupert by June and would fish until the end of September. It was always a great feeling to get home at the end of the season and look forward to a winter of free time.

Orion

Ron Bowen

One of my earliest memories is looking at a picture of a square-rigged ship under full sail in a stormy sea. My family lived east of the Rockies. I looked at that picture every day, without really understanding what it was that that drew me so much.

In 1973, I was working in Ontario and was offered a job in Victoria. I took the job and moved to Vancouver Island in September. By October I realized that I was now living in the land of boats! All kinds of boats!

One cool, misty day, walking along the causeway in the inner harbour, I watched a sailboat passing through the narrows, being rowed by one large oar off one side. As it got closer, I could see the rower: he had long grey hair and was steering the boat with a bare foot on the tiller. He brought the oar in, walked forward and nimbly passed a line through an eye on the top of a large steel buoy and

Making it tight.

tied it off. The boat slowly swung until the stern was facing me. Wood smoke was coming from a chimney on the cabin top. The hatch slid open, and a silver-haired woman appeared. I was spellbound and knew right away that I wanted to do something like that. A couple of days later I learned the couple were Allen and Sharie Farrell on *Native Girl*, living coastal legends. It would be another four years before I would meet them.

After that vision, I immediately signed up for sailing lessons with Ralph Higgins Sailing School. Ralph ran his school on a 1939 12 Metre (a class of racing sailboats) so this was akin to learning to drive in a Formula 1 car. I became a deckhand for him, day-sailing and doing deliveries.

That winter I got a book from the library, *360 Boats You Can Build*,

From the beach *Orion* launching day. Gary's boat *Grayling* in the background.

designs from 1930 to 1950. That's how I discovered William Atkin and the Ingrid, a thirty-eight-foot twelve-tonne double-ended ketch. I was going to build an Ingrid! That's all there was to it.

After a month or so of dreaming and scheming all things Ingrid, I started talking about it to a friend I had been working with who had been building a boat for several years. Although the "several years" part dazed me, I soldiered on, and I started asking him questions about logistics—building methods, fibreglass versus wood, and on and on. When I finally spooled down and gave him a turn to speak, he asked me, "How much money do you have for this project?" I hadn't really considered the cost, a bit of an oversight. Gently, he explained to me that I couldn't afford the cast iron ballast keel, let alone the boat lumber, the fastenings, the rigging and sails. Reality has a habit of popping balloons. This was a major setback and an eye opener. I was obviously ill equipped and unprepared to build the Ingrid. Time to rethink!

Dean Cariou, another workmate, introduced me to Gary Kolmus, who had built one boat and had lofted and built the moulds for another, a William Atkin Eric Junior, a twenty-five-foot full keel double-ender. A baby Ingrid! We met up with him at the Beaver Pub in Victoria and the three of us hatched a plan. We would build three boats with fibreglass hulls and wooden topsides. Dean and I had a lot to learn in a short time. We found shop space in an old freight shed in Victoria West, in the area where Spinnakers Brewpub is now, built the mould stations and strongbacks and got started.

We had to get all the fibreglass materials from the mainland. From a friend we borrowed a step van that usually moved supplies to a health food store. We must not have told him what we were hauling in it, which was three forty-five-gallon drums of fibreglass resin, five gallons of methyl-ethyl ketone peroxide (MEKP), ten gallons of acetone, and rolls and rolls of fibreglass cloth. We sure got the peanut butter smell out of that van.

We finished the three hulls in three months over the winter and hauled them off to finish wherever we could. I was able to move mine into a shop at my workplace, and by September the deck and cabin were done. I then moved it into a back alley beside where I lived to do the finishing. Gary launched his first, early the next spring, I followed a couple of months later and Dean in the fall. By mid-May, *Orion* was rigged and sailing. On May 17, 1979, I was headed for the Queen Charlottes [Haida Gwaii]. From the building of the moulds to sailing took fifteen months.

It wasn't an Ingrid, but it sailed beautifully! By the end of May I was in Desolation Sound. Early July found me in Alert Bay, where I met up with a friend from Sidney on his Haida 26 sailboat. He was planning to head north so we agreed to meet up in Prince Rupert in late July and head over to the Charlottes. The trip to Rupert was an eye-opener. Having only sailed in the Gulf Islands, handling the open water crossing and ocean swell was new to me. Also, as a new boater, crossing Hecate Strait was sobering, with some nail biting, but all and all an exhilarating experience.

My friend and I met up in Rupert. I ended up sailing for Queen Charlotte City [Daajing Giids] a couple of days ahead of him. After a month of exploring the Islands and seeing the old Haida villages and Rose Harbour, it was time to head south. By the time I got back to Sidney, I realized that my little boat was a capable sea boat but very small. I had to build the Ingrid!

That winter, I spent in Canoe Cove on board *Orion* and in the spring headed north to Quadra Island where a friend had a contract to frame a couple of apartments in Campbell River. By this time, I had convinced myself to build the Ingrid in wood. I started beachcombing that summer for usable wood to mill into lumber. I was looking for somewhere to build the boat when a friend, Hubert Havelaar, introduced me to Ron Woodcox, who had property on Cortes Island. Ron was keen to have a boatshed: I could build the shed, and in exchange could build my boat there. I spent the second winter on board *Orion* while building the shed. I laid the keel for the Ingrid in March of 1981.

I had met Dale Norland in Canoe Cove the first winter I lived aboard *Orion*. He had built an Ingrid in

Family boating on *JD Crow* with Helen, baby Claire and Lian.

the early sixties on a float in a logging camp up in Baronet Passage and circumnavigated the Pacific with his family. Dale checked in on me from time to time and provided expertise and inspiration when needed.

George still had all the lofting, patterns and moulds from his build with Dale and I was able to rent them at a very reasonable cost. That was a huge time saver. A friend of Ron's had a five-tonne flat deck truck that I was able to use to haul all of this to Cortes. Things were falling in place.

By this time I had made the acquaintance of the local machinist Mike Talbot, who years before had worked for Taylor Boats in Vancouver and was very knowledgeable in the boatbuilding trade. Mike did everything for me, from welding extensions on drill bits for bolting the backbone timbers together, to later on machining the prop shaft and rudder fittings. By late spring, the backbone was built, and the moulds were up. I could start to see the shape of the boat.

I had met lots of the Cortes folks. Most were tree planters, some were fishermen, and a few were boat builders. I was enjoying having lots of people dropping by and helping in the various stages. Roger Purdy loaned me a planer just at the moment I needed one. As there was no water at the boatshed, another neighbour gave me a huge wooden water tank that was filled by rainwater off the shed roof. The water was mostly used for the steam box. Another friend helped me steam bend the frames and a month or so later my neighbour helped me put the garboard planks on.

The building of the boat was one thing, and earning a living was another. There wasn't a lot of work on the island in those days. I found some carpentry work from time to time, cut firewood and did some tree falling so I was really happy when Ken Campbell, a fisherman I met on the trip to the Charlottes offered me a deckhand job for the herring fishery that spring. After that I had enough cash to buy the planking for the boat.

I had just started planking and Mattie Lutanen showed up and was keen to help. We planked the boat in twenty-two days, a round per day, no days off. All of a sudden there was a boat in the shed—quite a feeling!

Cortes in the early eighties had a population of less than five hundred people and a ferry that carried sixteen vehicles. It was pretty laid back: lots of dances, music nights, potlucks and just plain hanging out. Going to Whaletown on Fridays to check for mail and get the week's groceries was routine. Whaletown consisted of a store, the post office, one house and the government dock. There were a few live-aboards on the government dock. All the bush people from Carrington would be there as well. It was quite a scene. Dances at the Gorge Hall brought all sorts of folks out. The dock in the

Gorge would be packed with boats from Reid Island and the water-access people from across and outside the Gorge, all there to dance to bands like Bowlarama and the Valiants. One year, a local guy somehow got Doug and the Slugs to play the Gorge Hall. All good times. Some of the best winter dances were with our own Oldtimers band, waltzes and foxtrots galore, and an amazing amount of hard liquor. The potheads just couldn't keep up to that.

One day, a couple of fellows came for a visit, a man who had a boatyard in Finn Bay over by Lund and a man who lived on Cortes and had built an Ingrid over in Laura Cove in the sixties. They had heard about the boat and thought they should have a look. That was quite a visit. They left me with the feeling that I wasn't doing that bad of a job on the boat. I was certainly fortunate to have all these people in my life at this point.

It was late fall of my second year on Cortes that I met the woman who would become my partner in life. Helen ran a bus and freight service on the island, and I called her to take a power saw to Campbell River for me. When the bus pulled up and the door opened, I fell in love. Construction on the boat slowed for a bit. She came from a fishing family and had deckhanded on a troller. She was no stranger to the sea. Helen had a two-year-old daughter, and my life suddenly was fuller.

Between fishing and working off island on various jobs, the boat came together. Hubert spent a few days helping build the wheelhouse with me, a real shapely structure that required some very curvy glue-lam beams. Hubert had built a very nice wheelhouse on his boat, the *Grebe*, and I knew the value of getting out of the weather from sailing *Orion*.

Tad Roberts, whom I met while beachcombing boat wood on Quadra, was studying boat design and had a wealth of knowledge about hull design and sail plans. I had talked to him at length about a sail plan for the boat as I wanted to rig it as a cutter, not a ketch as Atkins had designed it. Tad drew up the plan for me, and it worked beautifully with good balance and a light helm. Tad has gone on to be a major designer, drawing and building sailing craft and workboats.

I sold *Orion* in the fall of my second year of building the Ingrid. Bittersweet, but the cash was welcome, and I was able to buy a diesel engine for the boat. I had originally thought building the Ingrid would take two years but the Cortes lifestyle and starting a family turned it into a five-year project. Come launching day, Lian was six years old and Claire, our new one, was nine months. The *JD Crow* was launched on May 16, 1986, and became a huge part of our lives, sailing the waters of Desolation Sound, South Georgia Strait and the Gulf Islands. We cruised to Alaska in 1991. By this time, the kids were in tune with the boat and took part in the daily routines such as helping hand haul the anchor as a windlass wasn't in the budget. The next couple of summers we cruised in the Broughtons and Queen Charlotte Sound [Tōtaranui].

We were on the *JD Crow* every summer as the kids grew up and every summer after. We sold the *Crow* in 2020 to a young man from Washington State who is a serious sailor. He and his brother were contestants in the first Race to Alaska, an endurance race from Port Townsend, Washington, to Ketchikan, Alaska, in boats powered only by oar, paddle or sail, which they completed in their twenty-foot open sailboat. We didn't so much sell a boat as adopted a wonderful family. The *Crow* is in good hands and has never looked better.

We now have an old fibreglass sloop we sail mostly in local waters, spending time with our old gang that seems to get smaller each year. Lian found my old Eric Jr. and sailed it home. *Orion* is in the fleet waiting for a refit. I guess I'm not done with boats yet.

Pulteney Punt and *Kaleva*

Will Soltau

During my early years on the coast I had several watery mishaps that filled my gumboots with seawater.

The first: we were running at night, back home to Vancouver from seining salmon in Juan de Fuca; I was on wheelwatch with another deckhand. We were in Active Pass, at the wrong time of the tide, and the boat was rolling and yawing all over the place, so much that the skipper got up to see what was happening and what was thumping around out back. He told me, the greenhorn beach man, to go check on the skiff, which was pulled up on the stern behind the drum still wrapped full of seine net. The skiff's bow rested up against the drum and its bowline was pulled over top of the net and tied to the cleat on the main deck ahead of the drum. All looked okay with that, but the stern of the skiff was sliding around on the back deck of the seiner as it rolled back and forth in the rips. I climbed up on the aluminum cap rail, sidled around the drum motors to the back deck and tied a line from the transom of the skiff to the portside bulwark of the boat. Then I had to do the same thing on the starboard side. I was up on the cap rail again when the boat took a big roll to port. I was holding on to the grab bar that went around the drum motor with my right hand when my left foot slipped overboard and the cap rail came up landing

My son and me, at our place behind the Pulteney Point lighthouse.

right in the middle of my groin. The unconscious reaction to the pain curled me up and my hand came loose from the grab bar. I now straddled the cap rail grabbing it with my left hand as, with aching nuts, I stared down at the rushing black water. The boat rolled the other way, and I scrambled back on deck. By the time I was able to stand up straight again and think about tying down the other side of the skiff, we were out of the whirlpools and steaming smoothly along. That was it for me. Actually, that was it for all of us. The fishing closed without another opening on the horizon so once we tied up in Vancouver the skipper called it, and we all went home after being away for three months. My first salmon season was under my belt.

It had been sheer happenstance that the first house that I, my wife, Heidi, and our eight-month-old daughter had rented when we arrived in Vancouver was next door to a fellow who was looking for a deckhand. When I talked about my previous experience as a crewman aboard a crab processing boat in Alaska, he hired me on the spot. Shortly after, we moved to a small ten-acre hobby farm in Langley, and I commuted into downtown Vancouver each day to get the boat ready to go fishing.

That summer of fishing had been grueling. I was a true greenhorn, learning the ropes, knots and my job as beach man under the tutelage of the man who had hired me. It seemed that, once we untied the boat from the floats at Menchions' Shipyard in Coal Harbour and headed up the coast, a change had come over my skipper. He was a few years older than me and an up-and-comer in the ranks of seine skippers. He had seemed like a nice outgoing guy at home, but soon became aggressive on board, shouting orders at all the crew. Maybe it was due to the stress of running an old boat for someone else or maybe it is a requisite to becoming a high-line seine boat skipper, but he did everything with force and little finesse.

We spent a lot of time fishing for sockeye in Queen Charlotte and Johnstone Straits that year. We repaired our net and reprovisioned in Alert Bay on the weekends between openings. We would go to the Nimpkish Hotel bar for a few beers to relax after work, but the skipper seemed to end up in fisticuffs with someone almost every time. He expected us to back him up, which mostly meant grabbing someone and holding them while he had at it with whoever had offended him that day or earlier on the fishing grounds during the previous opening. We actually missed one week of fishing because he had to go to court for knocking out someone's teeth. I was getting weary of this recurring scenario, so when another boat tied alongside us one weekend and the crew told me about the Sointula Salmon Days festival happening on the next island over, I decided it might be something to do besides getting into another fight at the bar. For this I have to be thankful to my skipper for indirectly introducing me to what would soon become my new home.

When I got to the festival, I spied a group of hippie-looking folks sitting in a circle on the grass. I got to talking to a few of them and heard about the old acreages on the island that they had recently purchased for very little money. Finding a BC Crown land grant was the reason my budding family and three friends had travelled across western Canada in our Volkswagen microbus in April 1971. I decided at the festival that I wanted to explore the island after the fishing season was over, so that day I found a small house in Sointula to rent, and in the fall we moved up and started looking for land. There wasn't any Crown land available, but the land that was for sale was cheap. We spent the winter on Malcolm Island moving from our forty dollars per month rental in town to a cheaper place in Mitchell Bay. There we met another young family, the Eakles, and when they proposed we go in together and purchase an abandoned fifty-acre property that they had located behind the lighthouse at Pulteney Point on the western end of the island, we agreed. It was accessible only by water, so we would need a boat. The other couple acquired a small, open lapstrake boat with a British Seagull outboard and moved to our shared property to start building an A-frame.

I had managed to find another seine fishing job for a couple weeks before moving to Sointula in the fall. Once I had been hired on the new boat, I was entitled to the same job for the next summer's fishing season. By the time the next spring rolled around Heidi was pregnant with our second child, who was due in August. We needed money, so I decided to take that fishing job even though it meant being away all summer. This time the boat was smaller than the first one I had worked on, and the new skipper was older, calmer and more mature. The boat was small for a seiner, less than fifty feet long, and we were a crew of only four. This meant more work for each of us, but the crew share would be a bit larger. The main drawback was language. I spoke only English. The skiff man, who doubled as cook and deep-fried our bacon in an inch of cooking oil each morning, spoke Serbo-Croatian (known then as Yugoslavian) and had a limited knowledge of English. The drum man spoke only Italian and Portuguese. Fortunately, the skipper spoke Italian, Yugoslavian and English. I could only talk with the skipper and had to pick up a few words from those other languages to better understand deck commands, etc. Off we went to the North Coast in search of salmon, and, despite the communication issues, we were an experienced crew who knew our jobs, got along and worked well together.

The second: we ran out of fuel one week and had to get towed to the fuel dock in Klemtu. As we approached the fuel dock the skipper told me to take the bow line and jump down to the float which I dutifully did, but the bow line was too short, and I ended up in the water between the boat and the float. My skipper witnessed my dilemma but with a dead engine was powerless to do anything. The skipper on the boat with power was outside of us and could not see me in the water. His crew was casting off our lines so our boat could drift into the float. I was able to quickly pull myself up onto the float and luckily only got wet to my waist. I put my wet gumboots in the warm, silent engine room to dry and put on dry pants. Once we got more fuel and the engine restarted, we were back in business.

The third: in the middle of July, we finally got into decent pink salmon fishing around the southern end of Gil Island. We started the week in rainy weather with a couple sets that produced about one thousand fish total. Then on the third set we hit it big and had to use the double fall on the boom and the winch to assist the drum motor with lifting the big set aboard. The drum man and the skipper were at the controls at the port-side stern, the skiff man was in the skiff, and I was at the winch running the line to the double fall and watching the skipper, who used hand signals to coordinate the lift. My eyes

The *Pulteney Punt* with the Morris Mini aboard, was formerly a herring skiff/ punt before we purchased it and built the plywood cabin.

were on the skipper when I felt my back foot getting wet. I took my eyes off the skipper only for a second to see why. I saw that my foot was underwater along with the starboard gunwale. The sea was over the top of my gumboot, the rail was about a foot under, and water was starting to run into the open fish hold. The fish already in the hold were starting to slide to starboard and the list was getting worse. I looked back at the skipper, and he was signaling me to let the double fall back down to take the tension off the boom. I flipped the line off the winch, but the boat did not right itself. The bag of fish in the net hung around the stern on the starboard side. The list was becoming even more extreme. I looked to disengage the still-turning winch capstan, but the handle was uphill now and on the other side of the cabin wall by the door. The mast, boom and rigging overhead were all tilting toward me and the purse line and ropes on deck were sloshing around in the water underfoot. I had to get away from all that mayhem. I didn't have to jump or dive overboard as the sea surface was now up to my knees. I just swam as fast as I could in my rain gear and gumboots away from the capsizing boat and the rigging that was slowly descending toward me.

Seawater was now entering the cabin through the door and making its way below. Soon the engine died and the capstan on the winch stopped turning. The skiff man rowed over to me, and I climbed aboard. We went back around to get the skipper and drum man who had climbed over the rail and onto the high side of the hull. They climbed into the skiff and didn't even get wet feet. Other seiners working in the same area saw the capsizing and came over to pick us all up. One seiner got a line on the bow and tried to tow the boat into shallower water, but as soon as they started towing, all the air that was trapped inside the now upside-down hull escaped and the boat sank. We were taken to a packer anchored in a harbour across the channel. I was wet from head to toe after my swim and had no dry clothes to change into. All our personal belongings had gone down with the boat and there was no chance of salvaging anything. One of the crewmen on the packer had mercy and gave me dry socks, an old pair of wool pants too short in the leg and too wide at the waist, and a plaid doeskin shirt. A float plane was called, and we were transported to Prince Rupert where we were each given $200 and a plane ticket to Vancouver from the Fishermen's Union Disaster Relief Fund. The first thing I did was to buy clothes that fit. Once we reached Vancouver, we were left to make our own plans. I had to get back up to Sointula.

The bright side of this calamity was that I arrived home about a week before Heidi went into labour. When the time came, we chartered a late-night water taxi to the hospital in Alert Bay. I was able to be there when

My troller, the F/V *Kaleva*. I was the deckhand onboard during the last part of the season in 1979. I started leasing it in 1980 and purchased it in 1983.

our son was born. I didn't have any paying jobs lined up, so I spent the rest of the summer at our property helping our partners finish their A-frame and starting to build our house. It had to be done. Heidi and our two children came out to the tent, our temporary shelter, later in the summer. That fall, our partners took a break from the property to visit family and we moved into their A-frame until Christmas when our house was far enough along to occupy. I still went fishing every summer but now as a deckhand on a troller. Our land-partner Stephanie stayed with Heidi and the kids while Kit and I were away working.

We upgraded our boat a few times, eventually acquiring a used herring punt. It served us well, being made of aluminum, with a flat bottom suitable for landing on the gravel beach, and able to pack a substantial load. We named it the *Pulteney Punt*.

The fourth: I did go overboard the punt once. I was alone but the punt was tied to our mooring buoy, so I was able to easily climb back aboard again with full gumboots. The punt enabled me to help the lightkeeper, who had been like a guardian angel to us all. He had bought a used Morris Mini for parts, and I ferried it from Port McNeill to the lighthouse for him. We could never repay him for all the help he gave us over the years that we were neighbours but bringing that car out was one small thing I could do for him.

After eight years homesteading behind the lighthouse our partners decided to pursue their musical careers, and we all agreed to sell the property and go our separate ways. Heidi and I bought a house in town and have lived in Sointula ever since. In 1980 I chartered the troller *Kaleva*, which I purchased three years later. I fished it until 2006 when I sold it and went to work for Living Oceans Society until I retired in 2014.

Raireva

Roger Purdy

Looking back, I realize that I had no clue how privileged I was. Ignorance is a blessing of early childhood.

Mum passed on to me the basic skills of navigating the intertidal zone and salal thickets, skills she had learned in her childhood summers in Howe Sound. At seven years old, my bud Bill and I were allowed to buzz endlessly

I did my very best to become a hippie, just as the real hippies were getting serious jobs, buying land and building houses.

The Lor Dell II. One day Oliver trolled out and around Cape Cook. With thirty-five knots on a well-established swell, I wasn't feeling my best. Then Oli sent me into the bilge to bleed the injectors. The diesel vapors brought me to the verge of puking; I'm sure I looked green crawling out of the fo'c'sle. Oli took pity, we pulled the gear and ran into the Bunsby Islands, the huge rocks appearing and disappearing as the swells rolled in through the tiny pass. We turned a corner into a flat calm, paradise-island anchorage. Oli told me to launch the dingy and go for a row-about. He would have shown me so many beautiful spots, had I stuck it out.

around the bay, each in our own family's twelve-foot Davidson dinghy, mine with a racy white six hp Merc, Bill's with a blue seven-and-a-half Evinrude, one of those big round ones. When we climbed forward, we could get the bow down a bit and gain a half knot; steer by leaning. Breakneck racing at six/seven knots, but we also putted for hours in the shallows, shifting gears, engine up and down, the rhythms and trickery of the tides. Then came the speed boats....

After graduating, setting my sights on a trip to Europe, I bought a '59 Chev Biscayne for $175 to get me to Pemberton where I was immediately hired by a small, family gyppo ground-skidding show setting chokers. ("You got cork boots?" "What's cork boots?" Shaking his head, "I got some that'll fit you.") That November, through a friend's dad, I got a working passage on a 20,000-tonne freighter, twenty-eight days, from Vancouver, through the Panama Canal (can you hear the jungle?) to England. Three months logging at $4.08 an hour paid for six months in Europe.

At twenty-one, hearing of older cousins and friends making good money fishing, I determined to get a job on a troller. Walking the docks in False Creek, I was taken on by Sointula-born Oliver Petersen on his Sointula-built forty-two-foot *Lor Dell II*. I didn't have a clue what I had lucked into, but I showed up and worked hard. We sailed for Winter Harbour in May, Lund, Sointula via Gillard (spun around in the Dents), Sointula, Bull Harbour, then across the Nahwitti Bar and around Cape Scott. I was stunned at the majesty of the straits and inlets, the power of the tides and the rawness of the West Coast. I cottoned on quickly and really enjoyed running the gear and pulling a few fish on board. Dressing and icing, poles down and up, stabes in and out, but I didn't have the foggiest about what the old man knew or the years of experience behind his decisions. Had I stuck it out, I may well have earned and learned enough to hook me into being a fisher. But the fish hadn't arrived yet, so, tired of scraping fo'c'sle diesel off my tongue every morning and longing so terribly for my sweet lover back home, I bailed.

Later that summer, an opportunity popped up to help deliver a Centurian 32 to Hawaii. I figured, *how hard can it be?* We didn't have a clue. Leaving Vancouver in late October, we were hard to the weather for the first twenty-one days, seven of these under bare poles, followed by another week surfing on forty knot trade wind seas with a double reefed mainsail. That trip helped me frame my mortality and gave me faith in mathematics. What a wonder to make Hilo!

Back in Vancouver, my pals had acquired small, ropey sail boats, primarily as party platforms. To join the fun, I found a lovely twenty-six-foot Atkin ketch that I could afford—*Raireva*, Polynesian for "Little clouds that indicate the trade winds." It was lovely to look at, yellow cedar strip planking on bent oak frames. Down below, I could barely sit up straight if I kept my head between the little deck beams. Finished out nicely, it had a tiny woodstove. The engine was a ten hp air-cooled Sachs Dolmar single chamber rotary skidoo engine. Shouldn't be hard to figure out. It only lasted a few months.

My buds told me that they were planning a trip to Desolation Sound that summer, and that I was welcome to tag along. That sounded like an adventure not to be missed. Andrew had a lovely old low, sleek British built thirty-foot racing sloop, the *Oonah*. With a full, deep keel and elegant, long counter, the water would slip smoothly over the side deck when heeled over going to weather. John had picked up an old twenty-nine-foot narrow, wooden sloop called the *Cavalier*, also deep keeled, with an oversized mast, a fifteen hp Johnson in an engine well and a car steering wheel mounted horizontally. It was a fast, strange bird. Al had the only production boat in the fleet, a Discovery 32. We were all single-handing, and they were way faster than *Raireva*.

Three days got us to Lund, then party central of the northern gulf. Over the next two weeks and many bottles of Silent Sam, my eyes and thoughts were opened to an entirely new cultural experience. Lund was alive with an amazingly diverse bunch of mostly youngish seekers of alternative perspectives. Some had bought land around Lund, some back on Okeover Inlet, some lived on boats at the dock, some were farming, some were fixing or building boats, some were fishing. There were still the remains of the Gulf troll fleet then, still a few coho to be caught on the evening bite. The dock was jammed with such a variety of amazing boats, not the least of which was the *Sailfish*, Zoe Roberts' fifty-foot bright red motor-sailer abalone dive boat.

Zoe, though small in stature, was larger than life. A few years older than us, she was a slender, attractive and very capable woman. She had two very fit and handsome younger deckhand divers with her. You could always hear her coming, and she could party us into oblivion. One beautiful, calm afternoon, Zoe rounded up a dozen or so joy-seekers and commandeered *Raireva* for an outing to Savary Island. En route, my hat was knocked off into the chuck. I stepped off the stern of my boat to retrieve it, assuming that someone would swing the boat round to pick me up. Zoe couldn't believe it. For the rest of her years, she would greet me or introduce me as the only skipper she'd ever seen walk off his boat. We spent the afternoon sitting on the sand, the warm flooding tide slowly overtaking us, drinking endless beer, raking Manila clams with our fingers where we sat, *Raireva* nudging gently up the warm sand beach. Paradise.

One beautiful day, Andrew came by to tell me that there was a big southeaster rolling in, and that they were going to take off to make it to Gorge Harbour before the storm.

Now.

I had no clue there was a storm coming. I had no clue where the Gorge was. Andy pointed to it on my chart. By the time I made the lee of Hernando, the guys were probably entering the Gorge and it was blowing southeast thirty. I managed to douse the mizzen and roll some of the main onto my boom, then headed for the Sutil Point can buoy. I watched myself get pushed toward that enormous rockpile. I was pointing hard to sneak past the can, the odd wave swamping the cockpit, waves cresting and breaking in the shallows. I remember watching a bottle of soya sauce fly across the cabin, smashing

Doing *Raireva's* bottom on the beach in front of our squat at the ferry landing in Whaletown Bay on Cortes Island. We set the anchor fifty feet abeam of the mast and rigged it to the main halyard, pulling the boat gently toward two alder poles lashed to the rail. France and I made a steady diet of the oysters from that beach. I sailed *Raireva* around the Salish Sea for two years with no engine. Just before I sold it, I bought an MD1B Volvo from Doug Goldman on Marina Island. Hans Croeker helped me shape new engine beds from a chunk of old-growth fir and Mike Talbot designed and fabricated shift linkage to complete the job.

to bits on the floor. *Raireva* roared in through the mouth of the gorge and I rafted up with the lads. That night I came down with a very nasty flu.

Two days later, the lads took off without me, but left me half a coho. When I came round, I sculled my Sportyak dinghy over to say hi to a guy on the beach. David Giblin was right in the hipster groove. Nice, laid-back guy. He was renting the cabin at the mouth of the creek for $50 a month. I offered to share my fish. After a very enjoyable meal and a mind-expanding evening, he said, "We're doing a firewood trip at Jerry's tomorrow, if you want to come hang out." I had no idea what he meant, but it sounded like a chance to check out some of the island.

We arrived at Jerry's to find a group of strapping, bearded, long-haired fellas sitting on a large pile of alder logs, joints and coffees in hand. Jerry and Lynne were living in the barn/shop where a gaggle of hippie chicks were making muffins. Soon the chainsaws were revving, clouds of two stroke smoke and chips flying, and the decked wood was assaulted. Mauls popped open the green wood and several trucks were loaded and reloaded, trundling up and down the gravel roads to various other homes. It was an impressive display of happy teamwork. By the end of the day, the pile of wood was gone. No money had changed hands. I had never seen anything like it. That was when my life took a ninety degree turn to the left.

During the next few weeks, I toured up through the Redonda Islands, through the Yuculta Rapids, down through Seymour Narrows and found my way back to Cortes. It must have been the spirits who helped me through the rapids and narrows and gave me a light northwester to scoot me round Cape Mudge. I had no idea how much grief these places can deliver. For me, it was an epic solo trip.

The Whaletown government dock was a sweet place to hang out. Friends on live-aboards at the dock, friends squatting ashore, Gary and Velma's store at the top of the dock, and a lovely ruisseau of French-Canadian gals flowing through, all anyone could wish for. There was a strong sense of freedom on Cortes. It was a serious challenge to the validity of city life. Life on the island was so full, and it cost almost nothing. I decided to stick around.

Zuk was a monster fisher, inventor, drinker and an insatiable worker, who played classical violin and loved opera. He always carried a can of tobacco, by its lid, in the tips of his long, leathered fingers. In Zuk and Margaret's living room, I drank mint and rosehip tea and watched him build four herring gillnets. We hand-bombed them down the hall and into their rusted out one-tonne dually pickup. We had an eighteen-foot punt, with one live roller, two very used ten hp Mercs, anchors and bladders. Zero overhead to join the gold rush. The three of us shared a room at the Maquinna Hotel, most of every day in the bar, waiting for the fishery to open. The bar scene was mind blowing. After two weeks, we ripped back to Two Quart Bay to fish in the Stoppers: we fished from six p.m. to six a.m., weaving through a city of lights, revving outboards and screaming. We delivered countless times; the whole night was a frenetic, maniacal blur. In the morning, I was handed three thousand dollars cash. That was the only time I fished herring. I have only recently learned that Pacific herring spawn annually after four years and live for fourteen to twenty years.

In the spring of 1981, I spruced up my little boat and sold it in Victoria. I then found my way to Prince Rupert to join John Helme, John Mohr and Finbar as an itinerant deckhand. They were leasing small, worn-out wooden gillnetters out of the North Pacific Cannery. Grub and fuel up, head out, fish for two nights and days, run home, party, repeat. The Skeena, the Nass, Dundas Island. Partying in Cow Bay, Salt Lakes, Dodge Cove. I was enthralled with the harbour, the river, bumping over the bar in front of Port Ed and Chatham Sound. I made no money but had a wonderful time in this amazing territory.

Back on Cortes, a squat came available in Carrington Bay, so I bought a new fourteen-foot Lund car-topper skiff with a new twenty hp Johnson to get in and out from Coulter Bay. My motorized surfboard. I loved swaggering about in my hip-waders and making it home on those frozen winter nights in the sparkling magic of a moon-lit low tide.

That winter, I met John Secord and his mum and dad, Cart and Anne, on Coulter Island and helped with getting their two boats, the *Orion 3* (a thirty-foot Deltaga with a Suzie) and the *Silver Triton* (forty-two foot Deltaga with 453 GM), ready for halibut. We ran to Rupert, spent an afternoon bluestoning octopus out from under some big rocks at low water, grubbed, fueled and iced up, and headed to Stephens Island where we anchored up and gillnetted bait herring in Butler Cove. Then started the daily runs out to the Oval Bank. They used salvaged groundline with gangions spliced in. Setting was slow. We only ran six skates, but once Cart sniffed out the school, John got the Loran fix, and we loaded up. Cart ran the gear, I hacked bycatch into bait, dressed, iced and cooked. Two-man boat.

Cart did make the odd excellent fish chowder.

Halibut fishing was two weeks on, two weeks off then, which put us out in some pretty foul weather, the boat sometimes pinned over by wind in the rigging, but not as bad as my trip to Hawaii, I guess. I had lots to do.

I jumped on the ferry, the *Queen of Prince Rupert*, and went home for the two weeks off. Cart and his bud were deep into a bender when I got back. John cleared out the last of the whisky and we headed for Stevens, me at the *Orion*'s helm following John, Cart dealing with his rats and snakes in the fo'c'sle. *Silver Triton* had disappeared into Stevens Pass by the time we arrived, but just as we came into the entrance, Cart crawled out and took the wheel to wind us through. Guess he had heard the boat sounding.

I fished the rest of the halibut season with John. We did well, so John took me on for the sockeye. The first opening lasted five days. After the first thirty-six straight hours outside of Stephens Island, we plugged the boat, ran into Rupert, delivered 10,000 pounds, then headed back out. On day four, I got a black bass spine in my thumb which swelled up huge and was excruciating. John told me that I was no use to him anymore and fired me. That fall, John and others were lost in a big storm off Cape Cook and Cart's body finally gave out. I didn't go fishing again.

Back in Whaletown, Al, who was making furniture for wealthy clients in Washington, let me muck around in his shop, taught me about woodworking and guided me through millwork for the Gorge Hall LIP (Local Initiatives Program grants) reno. Inspired, I left the island and enrolled in the Industrial Education teacher training program at BCIT. There my focus shifted, and I became a career shop teacher, another classic case of the blind leading the blind.

Finally, after retirement, a wonderful old cruiser fell out of the skies into my lap, and I was able to start exploring this beautiful coast on my own, my cautious confidence woven from friendly advice and all the threads of coastal boating from my early years. *Serendipity*, a 1975 thirty-seven-foot Pelagic trawler, with 3160 Caterpillar engine, is my magic ride. I feel so fortunate to have the freedom, skills and (so far) the disposable income to amble around these spectacular territories, guided by the weather, the tides and the spirits of those who have been before me. I am so privileged.

Rita Joe and *Juno 1*

Gerry Williams

I was born into an unusual boating community in Hammonton, California, a small company town. It was a place that centred around the operation of a few boats, bucket dredgers with names like *17* and *21*, which scooped the land of the Sacramento Valley on board to be washed, spun, sifted and spit out onto rock piles, minus the gold, which was the goal. They floated in ponds created by diverting water from the Yuba River: usually anchored to the shore by guy lines, they only moved as they chewed into the land.

When I was about five, my family moved to a Sacramento suburb called North Highlands, the civilian neighbourhood next to the McClellan Air Force Base. Families were large in those days, so there were lots of kids on our block. We were able to free-range a great deal of the time, as long as we did chores and didn't miss dinner. We had numerous fields, some creeks, bikes, sports and friends to grow up with. I spent most summers with cousins and my Gramp back in Hammonton, which was still a wholesome place to

In the wheelhouse of the *Juno 1*.

be a kid with fields, ponds, BB guns, bikes and some fishing and hunting too.

Hammonton seemed an idyllic place to grow up in, but in the mid-fifties, Yuba Consolidated Gold Fields Corporation decided to dredge up the land under the town itself. The houses were either moved to surrounding communities or destroyed as the digging commenced. So ended a joyful phase of my history.

I grew into a teen and after ten years of Catholic schooling, my parents allowed me to go to the local public high school, Highlands High, a treat for a guy who had spent the first two years of high school at a boys-only institution. I was very happy at public school. Even though I didn't excel academically, I was surprised to get a placement at the local college. I really took to college. I was also working at the local dairy, and it seemed like a good time to move out from home. I turned eighteen, registered for the draft, and got called up right away to go to Oakland for my physical. I passed the physical and was deemed fit to serve but received a student deferment.

I transferred to finish my undergraduate studies at San Francisco State College in San Francisco with a degree in Political Science with a focus on International Relations. I had ideas about teaching or potential diplomatic roles. While in college I married Joyce, my high school sweetheart, and a year later our son Peter was born. We were serious students, but we now had a family. I drove mail trucks for the US Postal Service during my college years in San Francisco.

At that time, I also became interested in photography and partnered with others to build a very complete darkroom studio and gallery. Joyce and I spent our spare time walking with our baby around the city, checking out the different neighbourhoods, looking out to sea and walking the docks around the Fisherman's Wharf. There were many simple pleasures to be discovered in that exciting location. Music was in the air, with many of the local bands playing free concerts in the park every Sunday. While an uplifting time, confusing and troubling issues were also brewing.

I had been following the Vietnam conflict since high school. I grew up watching war movies and hanging out at the base with friends from military families. I was a Boy Scout, an altar boy and a good student, with patriotic zeal. I shouldn't have become a war resister and felt conflicted and confused, but by 1967, I believed there was something seriously wrong about that conflict. My manhood and patriotism were questioned, but by my second call up for service, I was a war resister. I went to Oakland and refused my induction, which set off a chain of events that put me and our family on a journey to Canada via Oakland City Jail, Altamont, a winter in the redwoods and a journey to Victoria, BC, in our van, which we had turned into an RV.

We arrived in Victoria as tourists aboard the Coho Ferry and camped at Goldstream Park. After a few days, we travelled to Vancouver and were lucky to meet a family who were helping war resisters find a niche in the area. They let us park our van at their place and use their facilities throughout that summer. We therefore had time to check out BC and find a place to settle. When we met the Pickens, they offered us a chance to erect a geodesic dome on their property at Blind Bay, Nelson Island.

I had obtained mimeographed plans to build simple two-phase domes at a health food store before leaving California. They were simple to frame up, even for one person. While in Vancouver I gathered framing and strapping material from scrap piles at building sites. The dome was twenty-two feet in diameter and sheathed with hand split cedar shakes: the little cabin looked like a beehive. With a wood-burning tin stove and the propane cooking stove from the van, it was pretty cozy. We had a place to live on a knoll at the edge of the bay and we caretook the host family's place that winter while they travelled.

I bought a twelve-foot fibreglass skiff with a nine-horse Chrysler outboard, so we were able to boat across to Saltery Bay, where we stored our van. We drove to shop in Powell River or to visit our old friends, who were now teaching in Lund. While wintering in Blind Bay, we also got to work for cash as caretakers at the local log-booming camp when the crew flew out for a week or so every month. We also had the use of their yarder, a little tugboat, to commute to and from the campsite. That is when I learned to make sure the boat is in neutral when stopped. While I was tying up the yarder at the dock, the boat kept creeping forward. I was trying to make the knot as the line kept pulling out of my hands and then, splash, it was gone. I jumped belly first and just managed to land on the boat's huge rubber bumper, and crawl onto the deck. I had to calm down and focus as the boat headed out into the bay. After a bit of heart thumping, I turned around and tried it all again, this time, thankfully, while the boat was out of gear. This was one of many snafus that followed over the years.

Joyce and I still had to immigrate into Canada, but that process was delayed thanks to my earlier legal problems on induction day in Oakland. We met a family who lived in a house that was floating on the Maplewood Mudflats in North Vancouver and house-sat for them as they travelled. That was an interesting place: it was a collection of squatters' houses that once lined the waterways of Vancouver and the Fraser River. We managed to immigrate into Canada in the few months we stayed there, and were now legally living in Canada, but we didn't have a place to live or a real job. While at the Mud-flats, we had met locals who were artists, craftspeople, and college professors. Joyce and I got involved with the group who called their business Deluxe; their shows followed an eclectic, somewhat medieval theme and became popular gatherings of talented people. At other times of the year, Deluxers would occasionally rent a hall, hire a band or two and sell tickets and boot-legged beer. It was fun and used our creative skills, but it didn't pay much.

We did become the residents in one of the houses at the Mudflats. That house was attached to the land and extended out over the sea at high tide. It was a cute, functional little house, built above an open deck which had once been the work area of a crab fishing operation. The house, like its neighbours, had been condemned by the District of North Vancouver in a plan to fill in the area and build a mall and industrial park. As a group, we tried to resist that effort, but the houses were eventually demolished. We did get one res-idence saved for a senior pensioner who had built his house decades before. Thankfully, the area is now saved as a wetland conservancy. In all, we spent a couple of years living rent free on the Vancouver waterfront and had found an opportunity to make and sell our crafts and photos. We had enjoyed an interesting time, but we didn't hold our family together through it all.

I was pretty lost after that split. I was renting a room in a shared apart-ment when my friend Ross Garrick and I acquired a little ex-gillnetter to fix up. We got the one-cylinder Easthope engine running and recorked the seams, which were really wide. As it turned out, the boat began sinking be-fore we got it off the lift at Mosquito Creek Marina. That was the end of that project, but the beginning of being a dock rat for me. I drifted around North Van that winter doing photo gigs and odd jobs. One job was dismantling a pair of submarines in a huge shop at Dillingham Pipe, on Anassis Island, in the Fraser River. Ross turned up again that winter, after buying a boat that had been lying on the beach at Fords Cove on Hornby Island. Somehow, he managed to get that boat and its three-cylinder Easthope running and then across Georgia Strait to Vancouver. Once there, he hired a boat mover to set it up in the parking lot at the False Creek Fishermen's Wharf in down-town Vancouver, a bold move that attracted some unfavourable comments. The boat was a thirty-five-foot ex troller/cod boat named *Roach*, which was fitting, but thankfully not painted on the bow. Ross gave me a half-share in it—that boat needed a lot of work and, amazingly, we did it, until the money ran out, over and over it seemed. We were doing odd jobs for cash and even resorted to gathering old batteries and beer bottles from the docks around False Creek. Eventually, we were rewarded with a working boat that floated

Juno 1 and *Pescawa*, Ross Garrick's boat, at our floathouse in Simoom Sound.

and ran. We renamed it *Rita Joe*, the title of a play by George Ryga that was popular at that time. We had already moved aboard while still in the parking lot and became regulars at the end of A float for a few years after that.

That rebuild never really stopped, but the boat was now a stout little ship that opened careers for Ross and me. The boat had a lapsed B licence, and we were told by the Department of Fisheries that we could revive it if we made a fish sale by year's end. Our first trip got us to Bowen Island and back. After more repairs, we were off to Gibsons, Sechelt, Pender Harbour, Blind Bay, and finally to Lund, where I became proud and blessed because I met my future and current wife, Syd, who was living on the Sunshine Coast at Lang Bay.

The fishing season was getting on and we had not caught a fish. Money was slim so I took a job in a gyppo shake mill where I had an accident that sidelined me for a while. Syd introduced us to a commercial fisherman who was doing some fall fishing, and he kindly sold a day's catch of coho on our temporary licence. Wow. We now had a licence. The method was a bit seedy, but we felt that we had earned the chance. We had become owner-operators of a commercial fishing vessel, CFV *1379*.

I moved north to Sointula, hoping to learn more about fishing. I had picked a good spot, as the docks at Alert Bay, Sointula and Port Hardy were

Juno 1 with fresh paint and new bow poles in Simoom Sound.

really happening in those days. Amazingly, Syd and Peter joined me there and we did some short caretaking stints before renting the old bootleggers' house at Graveyard Point. Learning how to troll came slowly but we heard many fishing stories of enormous catches, usually reported in dollar amounts.

The next year, Ross and I fished successfully at Lund, then at Ford's Cove, Hornby Island. We finished fishing for sockeye at Porlier Pass and the Fraser River mouth. The following season we headed northwest, bound for Milbanke Sound. Unfortunately, the old Easthope was saltwater cooled, and the cooling channels were plugged by a calcium buildup. Overheating became a challenge for us, until that final day in Blackfish Sound when we limped to a government dock at Gilford Village and were graciously helped to arrange a tow to Sointula by a local fisherman. We found a rebuilt Chrysler Crown at an engine shop in Vancouver. That engine change took much of the season, so Ross decided to go work as a deckhand on a real troller, which he did successfully for the next couple of years.

It was late in the season by the time the boat was fishable, but the *Rita Joe* was reborn with that smooth-running Crown pushing away. After fishing for pinks and sockeye in Blackfish Sound, Syd and I made a trip to the mainland to fish coho. We cruised into the Broughton Archipelago where we found a semi-sunken floathouse for sale. We negotiated with a man in New

Westminster to pay $600 for it at $100 per month. With a lot of work and neighbourly help, we managed to keep it floating. Life was different now that we could dock right at our house. It seemed idyllic but dealing with tides and winds and wakes presented new challenges. Eventually we scored a handlogger's winch and used it to pull our house on to a newer float. We had a lot of advice and practical help from the hardy pioneers, including Billy Proctor, and newcomers who lived in Echo Bay and the surrounding area.

Fishing was good then and those inlets were productive. After a few years, we learned more and were making a fair living. We were well served by local fishing camps, where we could sell our fish and purchase basic supplies. In 1977, Ross and I sold the *Rita Joe*. He bought the *Pescawa* and Syd and I bought the *Juno 1*, similar in size to the *Rita Joe* but geared up to go a lot farther out to sea.

Juno was a better boat for servicing our out-back lifestyle, but the fishing business had changed, and trollers were only able to fish inshore when net fishing was open. Otherwise, we were mandated to go outside the blue line, which was a term for fishing offshore instead of the gulf or the straits. That meant that the Echo Bay area was a long way from the fishing grounds. At that time, our only communication was CB (Citizen's Band) and Marine VHF (Very High Frequency) radios. Syd was now home with our little daughter, Robin, and I became troubled by needing a change of residence. By 1981, we had moved to Victoria and continued in various fisheries until 1996.

From the time of my arrival in BC until today I have gravitated toward the sea. We now live in Sooke and continue to enjoy the sea and shore every day. This is a story about my experiences on the West Coast, but even more it is the story of so many others, the wonderful partners and mentors I have met along the way. I will always be grateful to them and interested in their lives and stories.

Sxwut'ts'uli

Harry Williams

I made four major kayak trips on the BC and Alaska coasts between 1974 and 1977. I kept a journal for each of my trips, now stored away in my sea chest. I only occasionally look at them. I also kept all my nautical charts. I don't talk about my trips very often.

In the winter of 1973–74, I was sharing a basement suite in Victoria and enrolled in a river kayaking course at the YMCA. A friend brought up the idea of ocean kayaking. I bought a Klepper kayak, a folding kayak with a wooden frame and canvas topsides, and storage room for camping supplies, suitable for offshore kayaking. I named it *Hummingbird* but used the Hul'q'umi'num' word *Sxwut'ts'uli*.

My first trips were in the waters off Victoria. Afloat, I immediately felt exhilarated and free. Feeling the gentle rolling ocean beneath and seeing all the marine life was amazing.

In 1974 there were no GPS devices, satellite or cell phones, tracking devices, or digital maps, but there were highly accurate marine charts, courtesy of the Hydrographic Services of Canada. I had all the required charts, folded neatly and stored in a waterproof map case. With a hand-held compass, accurate charts and tide tables, I always knew exactly where I was.

It really was about discovering the coast on my own terms, visiting the small communities and islands and meeting people. Being nineteen, there was an element of proving to myself that I was up to the challenge: a rite of passage perhaps.

On June 7, 1974, I left on a counterclockwise circumnavigation of Vancouver Island. Starting in Maple Bay, I worked my way through the southern Gulf Islands, and then crossed the Salish Sea via Ballenas, Lasqueti and Texada Islands.

Pressing on I went past Pender Harbour, and stopped at Cape Cockburn, Nelson Island, at SunRay, the home of ninety-year-old Louis Harry Roberts, a well-known boat and house builder, who was working on his thirty-two-foot boat *Chack Chack III*. He was a pioneer on the Sunshine Coast, and Roberts Creek is named after him.

Proceeding to Powell River, I raided the second-hand bookstore, then off to Savary Island followed by exploring Desolation Sound, Read Island,

Surge Narrows and the Rendezvous Islands. Following the curve of the islands, I made it to the Broughton Archipelago.

Just north of Johnstone Strait, I pulled into Clearwater Bay at Swanson Island to visit Will Malloff. Will, a logger, inventor, artist and woodworker, was proud of his Doukhobor roots with family in Southern Alberta and the Kootenays. He brought me into his living room, resplendent with guitars, fiddles and mandolins hanging from the walls. I spent three days there playing music, eating too many eggs, and marveling at the iron and wooden sculptures placed around the property.

In the '70s I explored the waters of the West Coast.

I then proceeded to Alert Bay, Malcolm Island, Sointula, Port Hardy and points beyond. When I was in the bar in Port Hardy, I decided to phone home and tell my folks what I was up to. They were grudgingly supportive, seemingly because I made it as far as Port Hardy without drowning.

The following day I caught the ebb tide up to Shushartie Bay, last port of call on the east side, where the remnants of a cannery that operated up to the 1940s were still to be seen.

It was exciting the next day to paddle up Goletas Channel and cross the sometimes-turbulent Nahwitti Bar. After crossing the bar, there was no turning back, but my boat had proved itself and I had food and maps. My confidence level was high. That night I camped at Cape Sutil, the most northerly point of Vancouver Island. Out on the water the following morning the open ocean felt completely different. The air smelled different, the light had changed, I felt unconfined under the big sky.

I was a little nervous about the strong currents at Cape Scott but rounded the Cape with the sun on my back, and sea lions and whales farther out to sea. I could see the Scott Islands andcould barely see Triangle Island, a nesting site for tufted puffins and other seabirds. Once around the treacherous Cape, I almost capsized in the calmer waters of Guise Bay due to inattention! I slept in a little cabin in the woods just above the beach.

August on the West Coast is foggy, so I moved fast to stay ahead of it. In Tofino I pulled into the government wharf and walked up to the local bar. The beer went down well, but the day was not over, so I continued with a belly full of brew. Feeling full of piss and vinegar, I paddled south toward Long Beach. With the wind at my back and just a light chop, I felt like a million bucks, playing and surfing amongst the waves. The following day I started early, but got seasick in choppy, steep-sided waves, so I pulled in to recover and have a nap amongst the driftwood.

I knew I would be home soon. My trip was still fun, but the most adventurous portions of my route were now behind me. It was a little anti-climactic paddling south, even though the scenery was great. I arrived home in Maple Bay on August 20. I had gained a quiet feeling of accomplishment to embark on other journeys, either on or off the water.

Pacific Foam with Oakland Fisheries herring skiff off the stern, Kitkatla herring opening, 1978.

In 1975, I took the ferry from Kelsey Bay to Beaver Cove, and then paddled north to Prince Rupert via the "other" inside passage, a route closer to the outer coast. I made a side trip to Bella Coola and hitchhiked inland to see the Anahim Lake rodeo and do some haying on a farm.

Past Bella Bella I continued up to Campania Island and camped on a wide, white sandy beach on the west side of the island. I brought the kayak well above the high tide mark. In the morning, the tide was low, and the water's edge was quite far out. I started moving my gear down to the water's edge, which took a few trips. After loading, I slipped the boat into the shallow calm water. Then, I saw a wolf sitting on its haunches right above the water's edge, a mere six to eight feet away! In all my going back and forth, I never noticed a wolf! How did a wolf manage to sneak up on me on this wide, expansive beach in broad daylight? The animal didn't seem threatening, in fact it seemed to be smiling, as though it had played a trick on me. I was surprised and unsettled, but it just stayed until I pushed off. We both went in our respective directions.

Onwards to Prince Rupert, I crossed the mouth of the mighty Skeena River, and then paddled alongside the railway tracks into town. With camping areas sparse along the Rupert waterfront, I ended up at Function Junction, a converted waterfront warehouse, where I ran into Paul Manson, working on a British Seagull motor. I slept at the Junction for two nights then explored the harbour.

I returned south via Edye Passage, Freeman Pass, Oval Bay, Kitkatla and over to Banks Island, from where I could see the mountains of Haida Gwaii.

In Kettle Inlet, on Aristazabal Island, I helped Kenny Olsen work on his fifty-five-foot boat *Pacific Foam*, putting in yellow cedar deck beams. This boat was originally a tugboat but was abandoned near Port Moody. Ken had salvaged the boat and was rebuilding it. I helped him for three days, but it was almost the end of August, so I had to keep moving. (I would deckhand on the *Pacific Foam* the following spring and for several years afterwards.) By August 31, I was in Queen Charlotte Sound [Tōtaranui], then weaved my way down through the Discovery Islands and then along Texada and Lasqueti Islands, finally landing in Maple Bay on September 12, 1975.

In 1976 I flew to Haida Gwaii and paddled counterclockwise around the archipelago. I started up the east side of Graham Island and found my way to Cape Ball, where I met the Walker family, who all played music, rock and roll style! I rounded Rose Spit and camped at Tow Hill [Taaw Tldáaw], then on to Masset, rounded Langara Island [Kiis G̲waay] and arrived at Lepas Bay on the summer solstice. At Thom Henley's cabin the celebration included Haida dishes such as: gow (herring roe on kelp), soapberries, eula-chon grease, halibut cooked between seaweed under a fire, salmon and salad.

I cruised on down to Frederick Island and camped on the beautiful beach on the Graham Island shore. Then, paddling to Port Louis, I crossed paths with Haida band member Guujaaw paddling his cedar canoe, with cow parsnip stalks he had just gathered for his breakfast.

I knew paddling along Moresby Island would be more difficult due to the cliffy coastline. The first part was fine, but I started getting reflective waves (ocean swells hitting cliffs) near Tasu. The next section of Moresby was grim—reflective waves, confused seas and nasty winds. I staggered into Gowgaia Bay to camp. The next day I had rough and choppy waters, but just north of McLean Fraser Point the sea turned into a snake pit and I was tossed around like a plaything. I got seasick. It was miserable. Then I got sick again, but not quite so gut-wrenching. Strength did return and salvation in the form of Flamingo Inlet approached. I picked my way through the rocks at the entrance and entered the calm and placid inlet. I didn't see any fla-mingos, but I did find a good camping spot. My welcome to Gwaii Haanas!

After a good sleep, I paddled down to Anthony Island [SGang Gwaay]. I reached Ninstints and camped for the night. The following day in sunny weather, I took a walk along the beach and found a dead sea lion. It proved too difficult to pry a tooth from the massive jawbones, but I gently pulled out the whiskers, which were about sixteen inches long. I dried them, gently rolled them up and stored them in a safe place. Upon returning to Skide-gate I gave them to Guujaaw, who was helping Bill Reid carve a totem near Skidegate Landing; he said he would use them for a mask.

When I left Ninstints, I did a night-time crossing to Kunghit Island, about six nautical miles. My main memory is the sound of seabirds all night long, mostly pigeon guillemots, auklets and murrelets. Then up the east coast of Moresby Island, visiting Skedans [K'uuna Llnagaay], Burnaby Narrows, Hotspring Island [Gandll K'in Gwaay.yaay], Cumshewa Inlet and points between.

By August 30, I had been camping at Rose Spit, on the northeast tip of Haida Gwaii, for five days in stormy weather, waiting for conditions to change. I walked out onto the spit and ate wild strawberries. Was I really go-ing to paddle a kayak across Hecate Strait, a place known to be treacherous in foul weather? It would be much easier to go home by other means, ferry or airplane.

Early the next morning, I woke to calm seas, blue sky, and a light north-west wind. I quickly took down my tent, prepared and launched the kayak.

The tide was helpfully flooding for most of the day. I was nervous because I'd heard so much about the Hecate and how the relatively shallow water makes for steep waves. It took nine hours to cross, using a compass for the first couple miles in the absence of landmarks. It wasn't a sprint; it was an adrenaline-fueled state of focus and steady paddling. The last piece of Haida Gwaii I could see over my shoulder was Argonaut Hill. About halfway over, Dundas and Stephens Islands, as well as the mountains east of Prince Rupert were clearly visible, and I knew I was going to make it. I made landfall at Roland Rocks and continued into Skiakl Bay, where I found a small cabin.

With autumn in the wind and a long way to go, I left this idyllic spot. I made Edye Passage the first day, and then down across Oval Bay toward Kitkatla, and then Banks Island, Trutch Island, Aristazabal Island, and down through the Spider Group and on to Calvert Island, all in excellent sunny September weather. Past Calvert it was over to Cape Caution, and the Storm and Deserters Islands before rolling into Port Hardy. After that I hugged the eastern side of Vancouver Island all the way to Maple Bay, thinking about harvesting apples back on the farm!

Those first three trips were solo ventures, but in 1977 I hooked up with a group of paddlers (including my friend Joe Ziner) and from Vancouver headed north to Chichagof Island, Alaska, with six kayaks (baidarkas) lashed to the deck of former fishboat the *Betty L.*

Shortly after arriving at Chichagof Island, Jack Gibson and I splintered off on our own. We decided to paddle from Elfin Cove, Alaska, down to Maple Bay, a cool 740 nautical miles away. Jack had to be back for school, so we made a beeline. We had eight bottles of Crown Royal to barter along the way for things like food and hospitality. We stopped at Sitka and Port Alexander on Baranof Island, and Hydaburg.

One hot day, we were drifting with the current close to the shore of Lulu Island, when we saw a deer foraging along the beach. We advanced slowly. Suddenly, a wolf jumped out from the forest and proceeded to take it down! The lazy mood of the day dramatically changed. The wolf killed the deer, and then started to eat it, oblivious of us. We slowly nosed toward shore. When we got near, the wolf slinked off into the bush, dejected. We decided to take one of the hind quarters, feeling bad for stealing the meat but knowing the wolf would still get its feed as soon as we departed. We only had a Swiss Army knife for skinning the carcass. We knew that it would be bloody as the deer was still warm, so we removed our clothes to keep them clean and proceeded to butchering buck naked, horse and deer flies buzzing all around. Finally, feeling like Stone Age hunters, we successfully removed

Baidarka 2, waiting for the tide to turn in Okisollo Channel, heading south toward Surge Narrows, August 1977.

the hind quarter. We transported the meat in a garbage bag, keeping it as cool as possible, but a few days later a marauding raven stole what was left!

On a warm summer evening with a flooding tide, Jack and I made a nighttime paddle across Dixon Entrance from Cape Chacon (southern tip of Prince of Wales Island, Alaska) to Zayas Island (near Dundas Island, BC) about thirty-eight nautical miles. When we arrived at the island after paddling seven hours or so, it was too dark to safely land so we tied up to an offshore kelp patch and drowsed for a few hours. From Prince Rupert, we hitched a few rides on boats heading south. Below Cape Caution, back in our kayaks, we were spit into Johnstone Strait where we had several days of following winds coupled with south-bound tidal currents and arrived in Campbell River sooner than expected. Upon landfall in Maple Bay, Jack had one day to get ready for school.

Crossing Hecate Strait in 1976 and Dixon Entrance in 1977 were the adventurous highlights of my travels. I crossed other wide bodies of water such as Nootka, Caamano, Laredo and Milbanke Sounds, but they were all daytime trips in fair weather. Now I have a family and a farm in the Cowichan Valley, so I'm not able to run away to sea in a kayak for three months. However, occasionally I do small local trips.

Dusting off the journals to write this story, what jumped off the page were the place names, so evocative, sounding almost like poetry when read. Lamalchi Bay, Smokehouse Bay, Aristazabal Island, Surge Narrows, Flamingo Inlet, Tucker Bay, Mia Kun, Estero Basin, Carrington Bay, Minstrel Island, Skiakl Bay, Langara Island, Skincuttle Inlet, Hippa Island, Blunden Harbour—for every place, a story.

Three Sons III

Tim Campbell

My early childhood was spent on a ranch in Alberta, miles from anywhere, without running water or electricity. Moving to the coast was a whole new dimension of life. Boats soon became a big part of new experiences. At age twelve, I was joining family and friends on many boats.

From a high school overlooking Haro Strait, I could see ships inbound and outbound from the Pacific Ocean. Then one day, at age seventeen, I found myself on the Norwegian tramp freighter *Faro* looking up at the school! The company policy was to not announce the next port of call until in International Waters so crew couldn't jump ship. The captain also retained one third of our monthly pay for the same reason. Crews never wanted to get stuck between two ports, with no shore leave or night life. This happened in Australia, when several Italian and Spanish crew members walked ashore, wearing multiple layers of clothes and hidden belongings. They never came back to sail. Being short of crew, I was promoted from my job as an engine boy in a hot, fumy, noisy engine room to ordinary seaman, with a four-hour wheelhouse watch of two hours steering and two hours lookout or labour in fresh tropical air. This then led to a quartermaster position (an impressive title but the job consisted of just steering the course the pilot demanded in coastal waters). It helped that I spoke English.

On a trip to Japan, we ran into heavy weather, which became a typhoon. The six-hundred-foot vessel felt very small. All we could do was batten down and jog to keep steerage for several anxious days. I started to worry when the old salts started to sleep in their weather gear in the mess room, not their cabins below. After off-loading in Osaka, it was straight to the shipyard in Yokohama to have deck and hull stress cracks repaired. And extra shore leave!

For eighteen months we shipped breakbulk cargo to and from North America, Japan and Australia. Later I decked on two yacht deliveries from San Diego to the Columbia River and Anacortes. I worked on the research vessel *Endeavor* out of Esquimalt Dockyard, then decked on the tug *Nitnat Chief*. I fished on various trollers, the *Lyra*, *Tam O'Shanter*, *Pacific Hunter* and *Arctic II*, for salmon, tuna and herring. This led to cash buying herring in "the Gold Rush Year" for Salt Spring Sea Products and Sea Food Products from Port Hardy. Not all seasons were successful. One poor season was saved

Warm water moonfish trolled off of the West Coast in the seventies.

because we were on the grounds and were hired by an insurance company to salvage the packer *Cape Calvert*, which had hit a rock near Nanoose Bay and sunk with tonnes of rotten herring aboard. The crew left the dirty job, but two of us persevered and eventually, we became business partners. That partner, Alan Meadows, later wrote a book called *Pushing the Beach: The Story of Marine Link Transportation and the MV Aurora Explorer*.

In the mid-seventies, it was time for our own boat. *Three Sons III* was a thirty-nine-foot Frank Fredette West Coast design with an aft cabin and a small fish hold. We spent months replacing some of the planks and ribs, and sealing the decks, with help from my wife, Judy, and friend "oily" George Martin. It was time to launch as refits can outlast the dream. We finally moved aboard with three-year-old, Marty. We had a C licence and jigged for bottom fish in the lower and upper Gulf. I would like it noted that we are NOT responsible for stock depletion!

I was looking for freight opportunities for the fifty-six-foot landing craft we used for buying herring. We moored both boats in Cortes Bay and Gorge Harbour. Marty was now in school, and would catch the school bus

Three Sons III, living aboard with my family.

that circled Cortes, often leaving from one place, and getting dropped off at another, by arrangement. It depended on where we found fish.

Eventually, the logging camps, tree planters, resorts, fish farms, islanders and the Forestry Service recognized our services. Before the Coast Guard had personnel stationed at remote locations, an auxiliary volunteer program of private vessels worked under their direction. When we performed rescues or salvages, the Coast Guard covered our insurance, loss or damage to our equipment and, sometimes some of our expenses such as fuel. It was a good system. It covered the remote areas of the coast and recompensed us somewhat for an obligation required by maritime law.

With baby Marina on her way, we moved ashore in Heriot Bay on Quadra Island, rented an old skid house, then built a house and worked out of Quathiaski Cove and Campbell River to avoid the "Moods of Mudge."

On a solo delivery to a lodge on Dent Island, I was busy running the hydraulic boom and doing both the hooking and unhooking. A guest came to watch; we had a short visit and exchanged business cards. In 1984, he phoned the house at three a.m. requesting help to take the luggage off his cruise ship *Sundancer*, which had breached its hull at the Seymour Narrows and was now sinking at the Elk Falls mill dock in Campbell River. I scrambled to get there as soon as possible and found the situation stabilized. The passengers were all off, but the vessel was partially submerged and listing badly, and the dock was destroyed. A salvage tug was tied to *Sundancer*'s stern, and I tied up to the tug. Some very stressed passengers were desperately trying to collect vital brief cases, drugs, and personal belongings. They had to cross my deck and the tug's to be escorted aboard by security personnel. The landing craft was too small to handle all the luggage, but the Coast Guard on site hired us to help clean up the oil spill with their skimmers and tanks. Thank you, taxpayers!

After many happy years of living aboard, we sold *Three Sons III*. (Eventually, sadly, it burned and sank off Steep Point.) Alan also sold his troller *Lyra* to concentrate on building a marine freight business to meet the demand. It grew from one small landing craft to several larger ones, tugs, barges, terminal, docks and ramps with partners and employees. "The full catastrophe," as Zorba the Greek said. Much to the family's relief, I now had an office instead of the kitchen table! As the business grew so did the regulations, overhead, crews, certification and administration. Al and I realized we weren't legally qualified to run our own vessels, so we alternated time off to attend months of classes: study, exams, sweat. After decades of working and navigating at sea without tickets, we were forced ashore into management. It felt like wasted time and stress.

The original small landing craft had a five-foot by six-foot wheelhouse with a fold-down chart table, one bunk, block heater, pilot seat and an old radar big as a hockey bag! Often customers would ride with their freight and sometimes a passenger would ride along just to sight-see where and what we did. The bunk was mine if we did get shut down. Food was made on the muffler, and water was bottled only. The head facility was overboard or the luxury of a five-gallon oil pail (lid removed at no charge).

On a cargo trip planned to take a day, a retired fire chief from Calgary came to sight-see. In the days before Autotel and cellular phones, communications were by VHF, not the greatest way to run a business. As luck would have it, I received a call for more work en route, which extended the trip to days. We did stop at a logging camp and tied to their dock, where we cleaned the staples, log dogs, grease and rust off the work bench in the boom man's shack to make a bunk for our passenger. Other times he slept among the cargo or in the one bunk aboard while travelling. When we finally arrived in Campbell River, we were both dirty, unshaven, tired, and hungry. I apologized and his reply was, "I had the time of my life."

We thought that if that man could have a good time without any comforts or schedule, why not provide passengers with cabins, showers, a lounge, a library, sight-seeing, walks ashore and visits to historic sites? Our idea was to carry twelve passengers along with freight. (Transport Canada regulations require a doctor aboard for more than twelve passengers.) We located a basic ninety-foot landing craft in Fort McMurray, which had transited to the coast under power down the Athabasca and Slave Rivers, with a portage around rapids down the Mackenzie River, through the Beaufort Sea. We commissioned a major refit in Campbell River and at the Esquimalt Dockyard, to use their big cranes. The superstructure was removed, the hull de-watered, the engines taken out and the bow section cut off. A new accommodation deck for twelve passengers was prefabbed, along with a mid-hull section and two sponsons to increase the beam and length. One morning we arrived for a regular day of work to find a crowd of CUPE members on strike, blocking the dockyard gate. Our situation was BAD. We had pre-sold passenger tickets and were under a tight schedule with our vessel in seven pieces, and sea trials to get through, all dependent on the crane operators. After a big delay and much pleading, the crane operators gave us one day a week, out of sympathy. They saved the program.

Another incident (there were many) occurred on a pre-Christmas scheduled supply run to Rivers Inlet, with the seventy-five-foot landing craft *Marine Link II*. The crew wanted family time off, so two high school land-

Marine Link landing craft rafted and about to load.

lubber buddies came for a "ride." The forecast wasn't great, but within reason;
the weather deteriorated sooner and stronger than predicted which slowed
our progress. We made a long bucking tack past the mouth of Rivers Inlet to
ensure that we would only need one downwind turn. Amongst other weath-
er-proofed freight was a propane delivery truck. My concern was the chains
breaking and the truck rolling or moving, causing a list. My poor buddies were
very sick, and I was anxious and tired of hand steering and throttling for hours.
We finally made the turn downwind and the grateful shelter of the dock in
Rivers Inlet. We tied up with extra lines. Tired, hungry, and thirsty, we hit the
bunks, only to later feel and hear a loud noise. The wind had increased, blowing
us ashore across the bay with the dock bull rails attached. The tide was rising,
we got off the beach and anchored. We are still friends, lucky break.

Another challenging trip was returning from delivering dynamite to
Haida Gwaii in heavy weather. The stove-oil day-tank on top of the cabin,
which was fed by the main engine, sprung a leak, leaving a miles-long oil
slick behind us. We were unaware of it, until a Coast Guard plane buzzed us
to make radio contact and instructed us to make repairs in calmer waters as
soon as possible. The result was a court date in Vancouver and a fine.

On trips with company aboard and hours to chat, I was often asked
about the transition from ranch life to going to sea. I answered that it was
basically the same: weather, mechanics and survival.

It came time to retire so the business was sold in 2017.

I was very fortunate to acquire the forty-two-foot converted wood troller *Marlaine C*, a Robert Allen design that Cyril Thames built in 1961 on the beach in Bowser, powered by a 6 LW Gardner and converted by Doug Barron in 1998. World-renowned boat designer Bill Garden commented that it was one of the nicest conversions he had ever seen. After several years (never enough) of living aboard and cruising, it was time to reluctantly move ashore. *Marlaine C* is in local waters, being well looked after by a new owner.

Dock goodbyes Surge Narrows, Cortes Island. Photo Claudia Lake

Glossary

baidarka: Aleutian kayak; a watercraft consisting of soft skin (real or artificial) over a flexible space frame

ballast: a heavy substance placed in such a way as to improve stability

brailing: lifting portions of fish from a purse seine net, using a brail or dip net

cork boots: rugged spike-soled footwear associated with the timber industry

dark set: gillnetter set made just before the sun goes down, as the changing light makes it harder for fish to see the net

fo'c'sle: slang for "forecastle," the forward part of a ship where the crew has quarters

gaff: a stick with an iron hook for landing large fish or a spar to which the head of a fore-and-aft sail is bent

gillnet: a net suspended vertically to entangle fish by the gills

gillnetter: a boat used for fishing with a gillnet; also, the fisherman on a gillnetter vessel

gow: the Haida term for herring roe on kelp

greenhorn: an inexperienced person, with little knowledge of a job or industry

halyard: a rope used for raising and lowering a sail, spar, flag or yard on a ship

highliner: a successful fisherman who catches significant numbers of fish

holystoning: scrubbing or sanding the deck of a ship with holystone, a soft and brittle sandstone used to whiten a wooden deck

in-breaker: a worker in their first season in the fishing industry

punt: a long narrow flat-bottomed boat, square at both ends, used mainly for pleasure and propelled by a long pole

seine: a fishing net for encircling fish, with floats at the top and weights at the bottom edge, sometimes attached ashore at one end

sponson: a feature on any watercraft that extends from the hull or other part of the vessel to aide in stability or to act as a securing point

stabilizer (a.k.a. stabes): a device suspended underwater from main poles on opposite sides of the vessel, particularly trollers and other fishing vessels, to reduce pitch and roll

thru-hull: a fitting attached through the hull of a boat

troller: boat used for fishing by dragging multiple lines with baited hooks behind a moving boat; also, the fisherman on a troller vessel

About the Editors

Lou Allison moved to the West Coast from Ottawa in the western migration of the 1970s. She settled in Dodge Cove after having children, working all over the North Coast, and living on boats and float houses with her partner, Jeremiah, while completing her English degree by the light of a kerosene lamp. Lou now works full time at the Prince Rupert Library and is devoted to all things related to books. She is the editor of the bestselling anthologies *Gumboot Girls* (2012), *Dancing in Gumboots* (Caitlin Press, 2018) and *Gumboot Guys* (Caitlin Press, 2023) with Jane Wilde. Lou also edited *Knots & Stitches* by Kristin Miller.

Jane Wilde moved to the West Coast in the early 1970s from Guelph, Ontario. She resided on Haida Gwaii from 1976–79 and, after attending nursing school, returned to Prince Rupert as a maternity nurse. For thirty-five years, Jane worked in health care in rural communities, living in Dodge Cove and Prince Rupert with her partner, Richard. She relocated to the Comox Valley in the fall of 2016. She compiled stories and images for the bestselling anthologies *Gumboot Girls* (2012), *Dancing in Gumboots* (Caitlin Press, 2018) and *Gumboot Guys* (Caitlin Press, 2023), with editor Lou Allison.